P9-ASB-619

PRESENTED TO
CODY MEMORIAL LIBRARY
BY
KELLOGG FOUNDATION

WITHDRAWN

YOUNG FACES

IN FASHION

Beryl (Williams) Epstein

Young Faces
in Fashion

J. B. Lippincott Company
Philadelphia & New York

72702

CODY MEMORIAL LIBRARY
SOUTHWESTERN UNIVERSITY
GEORGETOWN, TEXAS

COPYRIGHT © 1956 BY BERYL WILLIAMS

PRINTED IN THE UNITED STATES OF AMERICA

LIBRARY OF CONGRESS CATALOG CARD NUMBER 56-6215

FIRST EDITION

c
920
Ep 85y

CONTENTS

Decorations by Charlotte Alford

YOUNG FACES

IN FASHION

FOREWORD

The World of Fashion

THE WORLD OF FASHION, TO MOST PEOPLE, IS a world without physical boundaries. But in New York City, heart of the American fashion industry, that world is a small and specific neighborhood, bounded on the north by 42nd Street, on the south by 34th Street, on the west by Ninth Avenue and on the east by the Avenue of the Americas, usually still spoken of by its old name, Sixth Avenue.

There are about 170 tall buildings crowded into this little area, occupied by approximately 4,000 wholesale clothing houses. Some of these houses sell their wares in their own showrooms, to buyers from shops and department stores from all over the country. Others have no showroom and no designing staff; they turn out garments for dress, coat or suit houses which do not do their own manufacturing but have it done

1

for them on a contract basis. Together they employ a total of some 300,000 persons—enough men and women to populate a sizable city.

Garment industry workers refer to their world by the name of the street around which it grew up. They call it Seventh Avenue. Seventh Avenue belongs to them, just as the area around Times Square belongs to the entertainment industry. They read their own newspaper, the 40-page *Women's Wear Daily*. They lunch together in the neighborhood's restaurants and gossip away the last moments of their noon hour on the traffic-jammed sidewalks along which they hurry to and from work. They are proud of the fact that they produce three out of every four garments available in the shops of the nation's Main Streets. Together with their fellow workers in the smaller and newer manufacturing centers in such cities as Dallas, Los Angeles, Chicago and St. Louis, they dress America.

Fashion designers form only a small group inside of Seventh Avenue's working population, or in the population of any other fashion industry center. In most cases they do not wholly or even partly own the houses for which they design, but work for them as salaried employees. The distinctive ability which each designer brings to the world of fashion is accompanied by certain qualities they all share—qualities they must possess in order to achieve success in this particular world. They all, for example, have a seemingly endless capacity for hard work, and are able to do that work under the pressure of the rigid time schedule which controls the whole apparel industry.

The designer's year—like the year of Seventh Avenue itself—begins in January or early February. That is when fabrics must be selected—fabrics which have themselves been designed a year earlier—for the clothes that will be seen in the shops the following fall. After that come the research and study, the creative effort and planning, the false starts and new beginnings, which finally culminate in a batch of sketches.

By June the designer's fall collection must be completed, in the form of a group of sample garments ready to be displayed in the showroom. There they are seen by the thousands of shop and department-store buyers who converge on New York and other fashion centers during that month to place their orders for the goods they expect to sell during the fall season still several months away. Under these buyers' acutely critical eyes the success or failure of the designer's collection is decided.

But even while the buyers are studying the models parading back and forth in the showroom, while they note down the numbers of the garments they like and shake their heads over those they feel would not appeal to their own customers, the designer is planning ahead toward the next collection. It, too, must be produced at top speed because it must be ready for showing in the fall.

The pressure of this time schedule is severe enough, especially for those designers who produce four or five collections each year, with as many as fifty or more numbers in each, but it is more than matched by another kind of pressure under which designers must also work: the burden of responsibility each one bears for the continued functioning of a business that may involve millions of dollars and employ thousands of people.

YOUNG FACES IN FASHION

The women's wear industry today is highly competitive, with good material and good workmanship so common that manufacturers must now rely chiefly on style to make their products preferable to those of their rivals. Only good style can create the successful collection which will induce buyers to place sizable orders. Only good style, therefore, provides wages or profits for all those associated with any unit of the garment industry, from the head of a house and the designer he employs down through all the cutters, sewing machine operators, finishers, pressers, packers, stock boys and clerical help required to fill those buyers' orders. And the unsuccessful collection may drive a house into bankruptcy and leave many people without employment.

This dependence of the apparel industry upon its designers has given rise to a steadily increasing appreciation of those members of the profession who combine creative ability with a real understanding of the fact that clothes are now big business—the second biggest business in America. One result of this appreciation is the better salaries now being paid to good designers, and the higher degree of personal recognition given to them in the form of name-bearing labels and name-mentioning publicity. Another result is that the industry itself now supports and encourages the growing number of design schools throughout the country. In New York, for example, the industry's Educational Foundation, together with the city's Board of Education, sponsors the Fashion Institute of Technology where young people are trained for executive, creative and technical jobs under the watchful eye of the industry's own leaders.

Not all successful designers of the present day have attended schools of design. Not all of them believe a design school education is necessary. All of them do agree, however—this is another thing they have in common—that the broader a designer's education, in addition to the necessary training in skills and techniques, the better and more effectively he or she can function.

The final trait that all designers unquestionably share, whether they work in one of the few *couture* houses of America where wardrobes are individually designed and constructed for each customer, or whether they create the fashions that are reproduced by millions at prices that fit snugly into tiny budgets, is a frankly enthusiastic love of clothes.

But the application of that love, the means and methods by which designers transform it into specific ideas and lines and fabrics—that, of course, is an individual affair. It forms the special pattern by which each designer lives and works, day by day and season by season, in the fascinating world of fashion that designers not only inhabit but create.

Anne Fogarty

NOT SO LONG AGO, THE AMERICAN FEMALE DIS-
covered quite suddenly that she wanted to look like a princess.
She might not have been able to explain precisely what this
meant, since she had no personal acquaintance with real
princesses and very little with the fictional variety, but she
knew her own wish clearly enough to act on it, and she also
knew the secret formula for making the wish come true. The
formula was simply to buy several ruffled and rustling petticoats and to wear them under a full-skirted dress.

If she was historically minded, she knew that a quarter of
a century earlier the purchase of even a single petticoat would
have marked her as a political reactionary and, fashionably
speaking, an idiot. The American female of that day—this

one's mother or grandmother, perhaps—had recently won the right to vote and was dressing in a style that dramatized her new freedom. Her first gesture of independence had been to step joyfully out of the multiple underskirts which may have given her a royal dignity but had cost her long hours of slavery over an ironing board. In her scant new dress she had gone out to look for her first job. When she had children she put them into overalls until they were old enough for jeans. It seemed natural that her little daughter should demand chaps and gun holsters, or a space-traveling suit tastefully trimmed with electronic devices.

Under the circumstances, then, she was astonished when the young woman—her daughter or her granddaughter— wanted petticoats. It was equally astonishing—since those garments had presumably become extinct—that her desire could be gratified. The moment she was aware of wanting them, the petticoats were there, hanging in frothy rows or heaped in misty confusion in shops all over the land, as if brought into being by magic. And they had a magical quality too, at least in the eyes of women who could remember those earlier happily discarded underskirts, for these new petticoats stayed fresh and crisp from one washing to the next, and they hardly needed to be ironed at all.

Of course there was no real mystery behind the fact that millions of girls and women simultaneously decided to look like princesses, and were immediately able to satisfy that desire. Most of the petticoat purchasers knew the explanation. Any girl who was a little shy about admitting that she wanted to look like a princess could hide behind the fairy godmother who had granted her wish. She could say, matter-of-factly, "I'm wearing an Anne Fogarty."

8

Today almost everybody who knows that name knows something about Anne Fogarty herself. They have read about her, they have seen pictures of her, they have watched her on the television screen, and perhaps even seen her in person during one of the trips she makes from her New York workroom to stores throughout the country.

Anne Fogarty's arrival in Dallas or Indianapolis, to receive an award of some sort or to present one of her collections, is always well-heralded by a good publicity director. But once the designer herself reaches town, she makes her own headlines. Reporters meeting her plane on a routine assignment find themselves charmed into enthusiasm. Photographers assigned to record her reception discover that their chore is a pleasure. She is photogenic. She is good copy. And every picture of her, every story in a newspaper or a magazine, re-emphasizes the basic elements in what has come to be accepted as one of the real legends of Manhattan's Seventh Avenue wholesale dress center.

Anne Fogarty is not only the wish-granting fairy godmother. She is the princess who inspired the wish. And to make the legend completely satisfactory, she is the sort of princess who had to win her way in the world—a Cinderella kind of royalty rather than one born to a tiara. Any prince who wandered the world today, searching for the girl most perfectly fashioned to wear a typical tiny-waisted full-skirted Fogarty dress, would recognize this princess the moment he saw her.

Experienced fashion experts, of course, too wise in the ways of their world to believe in fairy tales, tell the legend in their own terms. "Anne Fogarty," they say briefly, "is her own best model."

"Well, of course," Anne Fogarty herself says, "I did start

out as a model. But that was only because I had to earn a living while I waited around for the chance to get on the stage. That's what I thought I wanted to do when I was very young—be an actress."

Wanting-to-be-an-actress is the real beginning of Anne's story. And its first, or Cinderella chapter, was laid in a little town outside of Pittsburgh, where Anne Whitney was born and brought up. She never knew her Welsh artist father. Her mother, left alone to bring up four children—Anne was the youngest—had a hard time keeping them all fed and clothed. None of them ever went hungry, but new dresses were noticeably few and they always went to the two older girls. Everything Anne wore was a hand-me-down.

To an imaginative child, however, this was more of an advantage than a hardship. Had her dresses been made or bought expressly for her she might have been afraid—and certainly would have been forbidden—to cut them up and remodel them according to her own fancy. But everybody agreed Anne had to do *something* about the clothes that were turned over to her. Neither of her sisters had Anne's tiny figure, which today is still a size 7 with an almost unbelievable 18-inch waist.

"I bought belts intended for small boys," she remembers. "And I belted everything in, very tightly. Even the sloppiest sloppy-joe sweater.

"The wonderful thing was," she adds, "that nobody really cared what I did to the clothes by the time they got to me. I had a marvelous time."

Then she corrects this glowing statement. There had been one occasion when she got into trouble over her clothes.

She was about five at the time.

"I'm not even sure whether I remember it myself," she says, "or whether I've just heard it described so many times by other members of the family that I think I remember it. Anyway I was going to a party, and I got all dressed up in my best dress—a pink organdy, it was. Then, to make myself really beautiful, I tied a red ribbon in my hair. When I came downstairs my mother was horrified. She had company that afternoon and she was especially shocked to have them see me in that unheard-of combination of pink and red. She ordered me right back upstairs to take off the ribbon. And when I insisted that I wanted to wear it—that I thought it looked fine—she threatened me with a good spanking."

There are, of course, two points to this story. One is the fact that pink and red, still a favorite combination of Anne's, eventually won the favor of the whole fashion world. Anne was already, at the age of five, anticipating what other women would later admire. The other point is equally indicative of her future: even the threat of a spanking, and her family's eventual and reluctant decision that Anne must certainly be color-blind, did not convince her that she was wrong. She knew what she liked then as clearly as she knows it today. But she got off on the wrong foot in the beginning by thinking she wanted to go on the stage.

"I realize now," she says, "that what I really wanted all the time was simply to dress up. All my life I've wanted to wear great full skirts, for example, and I didn't see that an ordinary girl would ever have a chance to do that—except, perhaps, at the kind of great formal ball that naturally doesn't occur very often. When I was thirteen years old I made myself a garden-party dress—a real traditional garden-party dress, mind you, long and floating and elaborate. And of course I never had a single occasion to wear it. But I knew that in plays, especially in period plays, actresses had chances to wear such clothes. So I honestly believed that I wanted to spend my life being an actress.

"When I look back," she adds, "I realize perfectly well that my only interest in school plays was the costumes and the setting. I fussed endlessly over what I was wearing, how the other members of the cast should be dressed, how the stage ought to be decorated in order to create a certain mood, a certain feeling. I lost interest when it came to learning the lines, to rehearsing over and over again. But it just didn't occur to me then that I could make a whole career out of clothes—that I could 'dress up' and help others to 'dress up' without being on the stage at all."

In the meantime, in between plays, she was racing through school.

"It's just that I was in a hurry to get finished, to begin my career," she explains half-apologetically, when people wonder today how it happened that she was ready for college at fifteen. "There was nothing remarkable about it. I just went to summer school every year, that's all."

And then she moved on to the Carnegie Institute of Technology, in nearby Pittsburgh, where she signed up for an ordinary all-round college course with a major in drama. She remembers a dress she owned then, a dress she had made to prove to the world how grown-up she had become. It was black, and draped so that only one shoulder was covered. Some years later this particular design would not have been so startling, but at the time, its designer says with an amused flicker in her eyes, "It was slinky—very slinky."

At the end of two years, still driven by her impatience, Anne came to New York. Her older sister—she is Poppy Cannon, food expert and author of numerous cook books—was already married and living in the city, and Anne made her home with her. She found a job as a model in a wholesale dress house—not a very difficult thing to do for a girl with her figure, her wide gray-green eyes, her sleek hair—and she used her lunch hours and every other free moment to make the rounds of the theatrical agencies.

It still had not occurred to her to give up her dreams of acting. She thought of her dress-house job as a stopgap. But even so, she enjoyed it from the beginning.

"I guess it's just that I felt at home on Seventh Avenue, right from the start," she says. "And of course I know now that it was wonderful training for me. Having clothes fitted on me taught me a lot I hadn't known before about how they are put together, about fabrics, about finishing details. And appearing in the showroom, parading up and down every day in front of the buyers, taught me a lot about the consumer's point of view. I was fascinated to learn what things they liked, what things they didn't like, why they believed a certain dress would or would not be good for their particular clientele.

"I've never had any real technical education in my field," she adds, "but those months as a model were a good foundation."

Finally the days she had been dreaming of arrived, the day when a casting director actually pointed her out in a line of hopeful young actresses and said, "You, there. Report for rehearsal on Monday." The opportunity he was offering her was not spectacular, but at least it was a chance. It was a role with a stock company planning a summer season outside of New York.

Anne hurried straight back to her boss and told him she was resigning.

It is useless to speculate what might have happened to Anne Fogarty if her employer had not been Harvey Berin, whose name on a dress, then as well as now, was a guarantee of good taste, good styling, good construction. He knew his business. And he had been watching Anne.

While she waited for him to dismiss her with polite regrets over the loss of a good model, he surprised her by inquiring suddenly, whether she had ever thought of becoming a designer.

"You're a natural," he added firmly.

Then, ignoring her startled look, he went on to remind her of things he had noticed. Hadn't she often said, out in the workroom where the samples were made up, "Wouldn't it be a good idea if the collar went this way?" Hadn't she frequently come back from the showroom, after the first wearing of a new number, and complained that she "didn't feel right in it"—that she thought it would be more comfortable, more wearable, if such-and-such a detail were changed? Didn't the fitters tease her about her acute eye? When Anne said, "This skirt is a sixteenth of an inch higher on the right side than on the left"—although everybody else had already agreed that it hung perfectly—didn't she always prove to be right?

"You're a natural," Harvey Berin repeated. "Why don't you stay on here? Go to school nights—learn to sketch. And my designers will be glad to give you some training round the shop. Think it over."

Anne didn't take the job with the summer stock company.

"The idea of becoming a designer had never entered my head until Mr. Berin spoke to me that day," she says. "But really, from that moment on, I didn't have another interest in the world."

Everything she had ever known and wanted had in that one instant formed a new pattern. Suddenly she recognized that what she had believed was a passion for acting was in reality a passion for the clothes an actress can wear. She knew now why she had cared more about the mood of a costume or of a set than the mood of a character's lines. She was aware that her feeling of being at home on Seventh Avenue was a clear indication that that was where she really belonged. "It all just seemed to fall perfectly into place in my mind," she says.

For a year or so her outward life changed very little. She did study sketching in the evenings, but she continued to spend her days in the Berin workrooms and showroom. Inwardly, however, everything had changed. Now she no longer carried books on her head, to achieve a poised and graceful walk for the stage. Now she spent time poring over fashion magazines, inventing designs and adapting them, and consciously absorbing everything she could learn from Berin's designers, his patternmakers, his workmen in the sewing room, his salesmen and his customers.

At the end of that year or so two of Berin's designers went

to work for another house, that of Sheila Lynn, and they took Anne with them. She had been hired as a model though she was promised a corner of the workroom as her own, and the chance to try out some of her own designs. But day in and day out she was kept so busy modeling that she never had the time to do anything else.

It was while she was working at Sheila Lynn's that she met and married the tall handsome young artist, Thomas Fogarty, Jr. They had three happy months together in their Greenwich Village apartment, before Fogarty went into the army. Then Anne, left alone during the long years of World War II, again had plenty of time to continue her education along its new lines.

She spent a good many evenings in the little shop of a skillful seamstress, Mrs. Bruna Luchessi.

"I went there at first as a customer," Anne explains. "I never could buy a dress that didn't need alteration, and Bruna cut my clothes down to fit me. It got so I just hung around there, talking to her, fiddling with my own clothes, sometimes helping her out. Bruna was wonderful. She kept telling me I'd be a real designer some day. And I'd always say, 'Bruna, if I ever do have a workroom of my own, you're going to be there with me.'

"And Bruna's with me now!" she adds.

But during those early war years Anne Fogarty's own workroom was still some distance in the future. Finally, disappointed that she was permitted to do nothing but model, and convinced that she needed a more varied background before she could find a fully satisfactory place for herself, she left her well-paid position for the first of several jobs which she

16

took thereafter in rapid succession. She was deliberately trying to fill in the gaps in her background. Each new job meant accepting a beginner's wage. But though her pay was invariably raised after a short time, she did not let the good salary she eventually won on each job prevent her from moving on to the next when she thought the time had come— and when she could find the opportunity.

She wrote fashion copy for fifteen dollars a week. Then, when her salary on that job had risen to about five times that amount, she left to accept half as much as a stylist for the fashion shows sponsored by a thread manufacturer. That salary went up too—and Anne resigned to go to work for the Dorland International advertising agency, as stylist for its Cohama textile account. There she was finally earning a hundred and fifty dollars a week.

"Oh, I was very chic on that job," she remembers. "Wore a hat all day long!"

The evenings at Bruna's shop, the long hard days on one job after another, were beginning to add up to a real education in the business of clothes, but sometimes it seemed to Anne that she was never going to get the chance to put that education to work. She recalls crying as she walked home through dark streets after a New York *Times* fashion show.

"If I don't get to be a designer pretty soon," she thought despairingly that night, "I'll just have to give up. I can't stand it much longer."

And then it happened, as it so often does: she was offered two jobs at once.

In both cases the opportunity came about because she was doing good work where she was, and because her experience with Cohama had brought her background, her taste and her ability to the attention of several clothes manufacturers. One offer came from the manufacturer of separates, of skirts and blouses. The other came from a new teen-age house called Youth Guild. As a newcomer in the field the head of Youth Guild did not know Anne personally, but when he approached Cohama as a customer for fabrics, he also received a warm recommendation of young Mrs. Fogarty as a likely designer for his new enterprise.

Anne did not debate for long over which position to accept. Youth Guild, she felt, presented by far the larger challenge, even if the salary was less than half of what she was then receiving. She left the advertising agency and moved at last into her own workroom as head of her own staff: an assistant to cut for her, a sample hand, and a finisher.

The first things she designed for her new employer were gay young ballet-length cottons. *Harper's Bazaar* splashed them across a double-page spread, in an unusual editorial salute to a new young designer. Anne Fogarty was on her way.

Those full-skirted ballet dresses were more than a turning point in Anne's career. They were the outward sign of the thinking she had been doing for several years.

She had not forgotten her childish desire to "dress up," nor her regret that ordinary people—people who were not actresses, that is—seldom had the opportunity to wear the sort of clothes Anne had once rejoiced in on the stage. One of the basic characteristics of the stage costumes she had loved best was the full skirt, long or short, that seemed to create its own aura of romance and gaiety. For years she had mourned the fact that such skirts belonged to another age, that they did not seem to fit into the life of the hard-working twentieth-century woman.

"And then one day it occurred to me," Anne Fogarty says now, "that the peasants of half the countries of the world had worn full skirts for centuries. Those women worked hard, too, I said to myself. If they could manage such skirts, why couldn't we? And I decided that it was just a matter of adapting the full peasant skirt to modern materials and patterns."

Harper's Bazaar, of course, was not the only enthusiast for Anne's first full skirts. Girls all over the country put them on with delight, and knew the pleasure of dressing up without looking childish and without seeming to have stepped melodramatically backward out of their own time.

One of the most ardent admirers of this new "Fogarty look" was Mrs. Jeane Saxer Eddy of Lord & Taylor's Young New Yorker shop, a woman Anne thinks of as "one of the most brilliant buyers in the country." It was Mrs. Eddy's conviction that teen-agers were not the only females who would enjoy Anne's clothes, and that Anne ought to be designing junior styles—those dresses that range in size from 5 to 15 and that are worn by youthful figures of all ages. Anne was delighted that Mrs. Eddy should think she was capable of moving into that field, but she herself was not yet certain that she was ready for it.

So Mrs. Eddy spoke to Anne's employer on her own account, and he agreed that Anne might design a collection of junior dresses for the next season.

And then the head of Youth Guild became seriously ill and it looked as if the house would go out of business.

"You've got to do that collection," Mrs. Eddy said. "If you can't do it for Youth Guild, I'll find somebody else who will let you do it." The manufacturer she called on, with this end in view, was Louis Kallish, the small gray astute man who for years had headed one of the large apparel houses. Mr. Kallish agreed to talk to Anne.

"I was scared," Anne admits. "I'd been a queen bee at Youth Guild. In a big house that already had several designers and several lines, I'd be—well, I didn't know what. Sitting in the showroom, waiting for Mr. Kallish to interview me, I almost got up and ran away."

But the dreaded interview with Mr. Kallish concluded just as Mrs. Eddy had hoped it would. Anne was told that she would be welcome at Margot Dresses, one of the units of the Kallish house, for long enough to produce the collection she had already begun. She moved in a few days later. And in a way that is the end of her story.

"Because that was in 1950," Anne says, "and I'm still here."

But since that time her name has become known all over the country. It stands for a certain kind of clothes, for a look that is gay and young and bouyant.

"Of course not everybody can wear my things," Mrs. Fogarty says quickly. "You have to have a waistline or they won't look right on you. You have to have what I've sometimes called a young figure—though that doesn't mean it must be literally, chronologically young. My mother-in-law, who is over seventy, has a couple of my dresses that she wears beautifully."

But Anne Fogarty is convinced that most women can have

good slim-waisted figures if they really want to take the trouble. And being clothes-conscious, she thinks, is the best and easiest road to this goal.

"You just naturally take care of yourself and your figure," she says, "if you worry about new fashions and how they'll look on you." And she does not think it is ever too early to begin this kind of constructive "worrying."

"I'd be happier," she says, "—though goodness knows my happiness doesn't have anything to do with it—if young girls paid more attention than they do to good carriage and good grooming, if they weren't so 'faddy.' Then they could be really outstanding without being conspicuous."

She thinks full-skirted dresses actually help a woman to move well, because the dresses themselves have a feeling of movement, "almost a feeling of the dance." And "I feel more rested, more gala, at the end of a day if I've been wearing a very full-petticoated dress," she adds, "than if I've been wearing the sort of straight dress some people think is more practical."

She never wants to give up her petticoated dresses and she does not see why she should. By now she has produced them in every conceivable material and to suit every moment of the day. And full-skirted dresses, she thinks, are a fashion classic.

"Everything that has a classic background can be modernized with a fresh treatment, a new cut," she points out.

She does like very straight things occasionally. "I guess I'm an extremist," she says. "I like things either very full or very narrow. In-between things leave me cold. But I do design some things for people whose thinking isn't that intense, who want a certain easing of those rigid ideas of mine."

She designs the shoes and jewelry that go with her clothes as carefully as she chooses the trim of a dress, and sometimes even designs the fabric from which it is made. The reason behind this all-embracing program is to produce an "Anne Fogarty look" that will always be a complete picture. And, because she is especially concerned with what women wear under her full skirts, she designs petticoats, too. Her earliest ones were crinoline, but she was soon able to persuade manufacturers to make up a new and more practical variety out of a nylon horsehair that requires little or no care.

"Of course they fold up nice and flat," she adds. "I took eighteen petticoats with me when Tom and I went to Europe the last time, and I got them all into a small case no bigger than that." Her hand sketches the size of the case in the air.

Their European trips do not include visits to the French dress houses. Anne Fogarty does not look for inspiration in other designer's dresses. She prefers to look at museums and churches and people and the way they live. And she is very aware that her husband's artist's eye helps her to see these things more vividly.

"I've learned a lot from Tom," she says. "Now I know *why* I like a color, for example. He has also taught me to use a sharp line for sketching—to follow through quickly rather than to labor and produce a studied effect. We don't really talk shop much at home, either of us, but just knowing him has taught me to appreciate art and all the things I see in a way I couldn't before."

Her appreciation of art in general has helped her to apply

22

the art of specific places and periods to her clothes. After her visit to Ireland she did a puff-skirted "Tea Cozy" collection. Another season she adapted the snugly wrapped obi of a Japanese dress to her own characteristic tight bodices. She designed a whole collection around a jungle theme complete to jewelry fashioned of big gold hoops or the shapes associated with African primitive carving.

Anne Fogarty says, "I'm very practical in my approach to clothes. I think it's ridiculous, for example, to own a whole closetful of dresses unless each is useful and usable—unless every dress is one you actually wear."

But one aspect of this approach of hers, practical as it is, proves once more how directly Anne Fogarty's life has been influenced by her childhood desire to dress up, and her belief that all women share this desire.

"I certainly don't believe in wearing an old 'good' dress for housework and gardening," she says. "I think every dress a woman wears should answer a specific purpose. When I'm gardening I like to wear clothes that were meant for gardening. Today it's possible to be suitably dressed for all the many different kinds of things we women do, and I believe in taking advantage of this. Why, I don't even like to wash dishes," she concludes, with one of her quick smiles, "unless I feel I'm properly dressed for dish-washing."

Understandably enough, in view of her own background, Anne Fogarty does not think fashion-school training is essential for designing success. She thinks its equivalent can be obtained, as she obtained it herself, by devoted hard work in one or more of the fields allied to actual designing. "All roads can lead to Rome," as she puts it.

"For me modeling was a fine beginning," she admits. "But not every girl is suited to it and it certainly isn't the only way to begin."

The most important requirement of all, she believes, is a really well-rounded education that stimulates awareness of history, of art, of people and of an ever-changing world, plus the alertness to appreciate every new sight and every new experience.

"There are ideas everywhere," she reminds young people. "I once found an inspiration in a chandelier, and another time in a pair of Venetian shutters."

But she also reminds them that isolated ideas can be completely useless to a working designer, who must produce an integrated collection of readily wearable clothes.

"There's no place in our business for 'show pieces,' " she says. "I don't ever let myself attempt the unusual simply for the sake of making a splash. New ideas are necessary, of course, but I think you've got to move slowly into newness, not plunge in like this!" And she brings her hand down with the swift gesture of an executioner's knife.

It is the kind of movement that reminds those who know her how decisive, how clear-headed Anne Fogarty is. It is true she looks like a princess, but she works today, as she has always worked, with a grubbing Cinderella-like doggedness, and the princess-look is by no means intended to hide this fact. It is intended rather to reveal the secret which Anne Fogarty has discovered—that "dressing up" is just as satisfying as she thought it was when she was five, but far more practical than it then seemed. And thousands of her customers, who now "dress up" for every occasion and every

24

audience, are grateful that Anne Fogarty decided to play out her own career in a designer's workroom rather than behind the footlights she once thought were essential to the kind of clothes they and she both love.

Jeanne Campbell

WHEN YOUNG JEANNE CAMPBELL AND HER HUS-
band decided to build an addition to their small week-end
house in the Long Island village of Westhampton, they first
sat down and figured out exactly what they wanted. Then
Jeanne drew up accurate plans. "After all, I *had* studied
drafting," she points out. From these they constructed a
model, complete to the smallest detail, showing precisely how
the newly enlarged house would look. And, finally, they
did a good deal of the actual building themselves. The
finished product looked just the way they had expected it to.
They were delighted. And they had enjoyed every aspect of
the project. So they began to talk about the whole brand new
house they would build some time in the future.

27

YOUNG FACES IN FASHION

Jeanne Campbell in Saturday's grimy work pants, with a hammer in her hand, does not look much like the smartly suited Jeanne Campbell who appears each weekday morning at Sportwhirl, the New York sportswear house for which she designs. But she is a far more consistent person than the two sharply different pictures suggest. Jeanne planned ahead toward her career from the time she was a little girl. She has never been afraid of hard work. Her small trim figure, with its bouncing horsetail of skinned-back brown hair, is still alive with energy at the end of a long day. And the amused look in her eyes tells you that she has a lot of fun turning out her characteristically fresh, gay, easy-to-wear clothes—clothes which won her the Fashion Critics' Coty Award in 1955. Furthermore, she enjoys the clothes themselves when they are finished, and the completion of each collection leaves her impatient and eager to get on with the next. In other words, her success as a designer stems from exactly the same qualities that made her a cheerful and efficient partner in the Campbells' private construction enterprise.

It is true that Jeanne was not clear from the very start about what she wanted to do. She wasn't crying for a sketch pad in her cradle. When she was eight years old, in fact, she was quite sure that she would be a violinist when she grew up. Her parents let her take lessons and she practised pretty faithfully for two whole years. But in the meantime she was becoming steadily more curious about art—about painting and drawing in general, and about sketching clothes in particular—and finally she asked her mother if she might not study with a young artist living in the neighborhood.

The answer was yes, if Jeanne preferred that to the violin. She could have lessons in either subject she chose, her mother said, but she couldn't have both. So at the ripe age of ten Jeanne made up her mind, permanently. And from then on, when grownups asked that inevitable "What are you going to be when you're a big girl, Jeanne?" she had a ready and unchanging answer: she was going to be a designer.

She had to wait until she was twenty-six, and already Mrs. Edward A. Campbell, to land her first real professional designing job. The interval had seemed painfully long to her, but she had always felt sure it would end sometime, and satisfactorily. And everything she did during those sixteen years would prove useful to the kind of work she knew she would eventually be doing.

Certainly one reason why the sportswear Jeanne designs today is adaptable to city wear, to farm-country life, and to the sunniest sandiest seashore, is because she has lived at the shore and on a farm and in cities as different as Washington and New York. While she played and worked in those different environments she was constantly aware of the kind of clothes she found most wearable in each. Today she translates that awareness into clothes that have proved particularly popular with girls who, like herself, want to be comfortably, attractively dressed for every moment of their busy and varied lives.

Jeanne Sanford Campbell began dividing her time between the shore and the country during her childhood, when she lived half of each year on a Pennsylvania farm and half in the town of Clearwater on Florida's west coast.

The farm belonged to her father, J. H. Sanford, who had

purchased his 166 acres in the South Hills country not far from Pittsburgh after he retired from an active career in the coal industry. Cows were Mr. Sanford's special hobby, but there was one horse for the amusement of the three Sanford children and plenty of space for them to ride. The thing Jeanne remembers best about the horse is the way her brother would help her to mount it, and then whack the animal's flank to send him off at a wild gallop. "He wanted to train it to be a real Wild West horse," she explains. "I guess he just took for granted I'd manage to hold on somehow."

But Mr. Sanford found a gentleman's farm too quiet and inactive a place once the cold weather set in each year, and he usually took off then for Mexico on a rambling search for potential oil fields or workable silver mines. Mrs. Sanford, although much younger than her husband, was not equally enthusiastic about such rugged jaunts and definitely disapproved of them for her children. She did agree, though, that southern sunshine was preferable to a snow-bound northern winter. And so she bought what the family always referred to as "mother's house," in the small town west of Tampa.

After that the Sanford children—Jeanne and her brother and sister, both older than herself—attended classes every September in the small school near the farm. But a little later, when the leaves had turned and fallen, they and their parents packed themselves into a car, along with the family dog, and headed south. A week afterward the youngsters were resuming their interrupted education in the Clearwater school, where they remained until spring.

Jeanne enjoyed this back-and-forth existence as much as most children would. But when she was ready to enter Mt.

Lebanon High School it was decided that she ought to remain on the farm all year. That arrangement had its advantages, too, for Jeanne. She promptly signed up for a Saturday art course.

By that time she owned a real artist's easel, mounted on a professional-looking stand, and she was taking her art studies very seriously. Her early lessons with the young artist who lived a few miles away from the farm had taught Jeanne the rudiments of painting in oil and water colors. But now that she could get into Pittsburgh every Saturday by bus, she attended the life-sketching classes at the Pittsburgh Art Institute. And as soon as school closed each summer she went to the Institute every day and took all the courses it offered in fashion art.

Jeanne wished, as her high-school graduation neared, that she could go to a college where she might major in fashion design.

"If I had it to do over again now," Jeanne says, "I'd be able to do that. I think the Rhode Island School of Design, for example, now gives exactly the sort of thing I wanted— a good well-rounded education plus training in design. That's the kind of education I think designers ought to have. You can't be a good designer unless you're a well-rounded person."

But at the time when Jeanne was ready for college, no such curriculum as she wanted was available. The Pittsburgh Art Institute, however, was just inaugurating a new one-year course in designing, and Jeanne finally decided to take it rather than attend a college where she could obtain little or no training in her chosen field.

At the end of the course her teachers, delighted with her

31

CODY MEMORIAL LIBRARY
SOUTHWESTERN UNIVERSITY
GEORGETOWN, TEXAS

72702

work, asked her to remain on at the Institute as an instructor. Jeanne agreed. She taught classes during the day, and evening classes too. "It was rugged," she admits. And although she was invited to stay on for a second year, she refused that offer. It wasn't that she was afraid of the hard work. It was just that she was eager to get out into the world and find a job for herself in the clothes-producing industry.

"Of course," she says, "if I had known then what I know now, I'd have realized how incomplete my education was. One year of training just isn't enough. Oh, I could sketch all right. And it's true I was pretty good at cutting and at making patterns. But so far as practical experience goes—well, that takes a long time."

But it was Jeanne's mother—Mr. Sanford had died a few years before—who prevented her from starting off for New York to look for a job. Mrs. Sanford insisted that a girl just two years out of high school was still too young for that kind of venture. And then she suggested another plan which in some ways sounded even more attractive to an ambitious twenty-year-old. She offered to finance a small dress shop in Clearwater.

It was fun getting the shop ready. Mrs. Sanford, who had always enjoyed experimenting with decorating problems, worked along with her daughter every day. They were both pleased with the way things looked on the day the shop opened in the autumn of 1939.

Jeanne herself had made up several items of sportswear to display to her first customers. "I still think some of them were cute," she says. "I remember a one-piece play suit that would still be good today, I believe." But the bulk of her stock had been supplied through a professional buyer in New York who, as usual in such circumstances, had made her own selections from the city's wholesale market.

People began to drop in almost as soon as the doors were open. Naturally Jeanne was pleased if they liked her own things, and they did. But she also realized very soon that, no matter what they bought, they could give her invaluable hints on fashion prejudices and fashion preferences. Most of them had come to Florida for the season from all over the country, and they were a good cross section of a future designer's potential customers. By talking to them and listening to them Jeanne acquired a new understanding of why a woman will choose one dress rather than another, what makes her feel at ease and what makes her uncomfortable. A retail shop, Jeanne was discovering, was more than a showcase for her own few models. It was also a classroom where she could continue her education.

Within a few weeks Jeanne knew that not all the New York buyer's choices had been wise, and she was beginning to be explicit about the orders she sent north. Once she even went to New York herself and accompanied the buyer on her rounds from showroom to showroom, making her own decisions about the clothes she thought she could sell in Clearwater.

But the trip was as unsettling as it was exciting. It made Jeanne impatient to move closer to her goal of being a working designer. Though the shop was doing well enough, and was providing a good training ground in many ways, Jeanne knew that she wasn't going to be satisfied with it much longer. She didn't intend to spend her life selling clothes other people had made. And the shop was not giving her the chance she had hoped for to make up her own original designs.

A Florida dress manufacturer—Jeanne suspects that his Miami plant was the only one in the state at that time—did suggest that she open her own factory, but Jeanne knew she was not ready to do that. And yet without a wholesale manufacturing setup she could not produce her own things in profitable quantities. For the most part, therefore, she had been unable to make up her own designs except on a special-order basis.

"If someone walked into the shop and said she wanted a white sports dress, and I didn't have one in stock—well, of course I said right away that I could design one just for her and make it up," Jeanne explains. "And once in a while I got a chance to do that. But the difficulty was that most of our customers were in Florida on vacation, and expecting to move on in a few days, so naturally they didn't have time to wait around for a dress to be custom designed and made up and fitted and all."

Mrs. Sanford and her daughter closed up the shop at the end of about a year, and together they went back north. Jeanne's mother still thought her daughter was not yet old enough to make a one-girl assault on New York, so they settled down on the farm again and Jeanne began spending her days in Pittsburgh, hunting for a job there.

There was not a working designer in the city then, and only a single dress manufacturer. Jeanne finally went to work, a little grimly, in the display section of Kaufman's, the big Pittsburgh department store.

"But that was excellent training, too," she says now. The

designing and construction of counter and window displays—out of paper, fabric, metal and hundreds of ingeniously utilized odds and ends—developed a good eye, a fine color sense, and a flair for eye-catching appeal. Devising and putting together a charming background for a group of mannequins wearing new spring suits demanded first a careful study of those suits, and a comprehension of why a customer was going to like them and what aspects of them the customer was going to like best.

The display job, however, like the retail shop, could not be an end in itself so far as Jeanne was concerned. After a time she felt she had learned all she was likely to learn there, and she became restless to move on, to get closer to her actual goal. On the other hand, since the United States had just become involved in World War II, she was not at all certain of what she ought to try next. Like many other young people at that time she was half convinced that she had no right to think of her own career at all, when posters on every side urged her to join the WACs or some similar organization.

The situation solved itself for Jeanne when, on a visit to Florida with her mother, she met Edward A. Campbell, stationed temporarily at an air base near Clearwater. They became engaged shortly afterward, in what Jeanne describes as highly unoriginal circumstances. The club veranda corner where the event took place was so popular a spot for such avowals—Jeanne's sister became engaged there too, and so did several of her friends—that the club owner declared he would erect a plaque to commemorate the numerous romances that particular corner had witnessed. When young

Campbell left the country shortly thereafter, on an overseas assignment, Jeanne went to Washington to draw maps and charts for the Civil Aeronautics Administration, and continued to work for the government until Campbell was assigned to duty in the United States in 1944 and they could be married.

They spent the first months of their marriage, as so many young couples did during wartime, traveling from air base to air base. But finally Campbell was assigned to a job at a Brooklyn military installation, and they could settle down to make a home for themselves in New York. Jeanne started out immediately on the Seventh-Avenue job hunt she had long wanted to undertake. It didn't last long. Within a few weeks she was hired as a designer by Loomtogs, a sportswear house.

"I guess I just talked my way in," she says.

She learned later that Loomtogs had previously retained its designers for brief periods only, sometimes merely long enough to prepare a single season's line. But in Jeanne's case they kept her on, season after season. "The salary wasn't very high and maybe that's one reason why they thought it was worth while to gamble on me," Jeanne herself says. But her employers must have realized fairly soon that this particular young designer was not a very dubious gamble. Buyers liked her clothes and bought them in steadily increasing numbers. And in 1951, toward the end of Jeanne's fifth year with the company, the originality and quality of the designs she had produced there won her *Mademoiselle's* Merit Award in Fashion.

But when Jeanne first went to work for Loomtogs she

was aware only that the job called for every bit of technical ability she possessed, in addition to any skill she might prove to have as a creative designer in the mass-production field. Since there was only one sample maker in the big Loomtogs workroom, Jeanne herself often had to translate her sketches into made-up dresses, and to work closely with the patternmaker until her original idea was transformed into a product that could be profitably duplicated by the dozen or by the gross.

Summer clothes were the chief output of Loomtogs, preceded by a small line of late-winter cruise clothes and followed by a small line of fall sportswear in fabrics such as jersey and corduroy.

"It was a good time to be getting into sportswear," Jeanne explains, as if half-apologizing for her quick success. "It was the moment when casual sports clothes were beginning to mean more than they ever had before—when they were coming to have some of the importance they have today."

Jeanne had always led an active life herself, swimming, riding and playing tennis, shuttling back and forth between the farm and Florida, dashing to the Art Institute classes by suburban bus, running her own shop, and traveling around the country under the crowded and difficult conditions of wartime trains and hotels. She knew what kind of clothes stood up under those circumstances. She knew which materials would hold up well during a long journey, which cut would produce a dress likely to keep its shape in spite of hard wear. As a practical girl herself, she liked practical clothes. But she also liked clothes to be gay, and she saw no reason why the two qualities could not be combined. She was soon proving how well she herself could combine them.

Mademoiselle's citation of her particularly pointed out another aspect of her skill at combining two qualities, when it declared that Jeanne Campbell "has proved by her own ingenuity that high fashion and low prices can be synonymous." And the citation concluded that "with her inventive denims, her combination of fabrics like organdy and jersey, her far-ahead use of tapered pants, really full skirts and 'glamour separates,' she has endeared herself to all devotees of young, easy casualness."

But by the time the magazine appeared bearing announcement of that award Jeanne had been invited to join Sportwhirl and she had become the new designer of that house, as successor to Lorraine Budny whom Jeanne had known for some time.

Sportwhirl was and is a house devoted to the production of those clothes referred to in the trade, and in the fashion magazines, as "separates." Originally the word referred chiefly to skirts-and-blouses or sweaters-and-skirts of the purely sports variety. But Jeanne has helped the word's meaning to grow until now a wearer of her separates can be suitably dressed for almost any conceivable occasion from an early morning class or supermarket shopping trip to a formal evening affair. She has also added to her line a few one-piece dresses, together with suits and coats, but its basic is still those separates which form the backbone of so many American wardrobes.

Jeanne has sometimes had difficulty explaining just what separates are or can be, particularly when she is answering the questions of her friends' husbands. These puzzled males, like thousands of other husbands everywhere, had finally and proudly assimilated the word "separates" into their own vocabularies, so that when their wives wore blouse-and-skirt combinations they could refer to them glibly by that term. But when they heard women apply the same word to a luscious length of evening skirt climaxed by a brief bare bodice, they were likely to stare incredulously and demand, "That's a separate, too?"

"Those are separates," Jeanne would correct them patiently. "Separate top and bottom—that's all there is to it really. And there's no reason why the two things can't make up into formal evening wear as well as into something for a long country walk."

One of the few times her job really scared her, even with five years of successful designing already in her background, was when she was first asked to produce a group of dressy holiday separates for Sportwhirl. The reason for her fear was not that she could not visualize the "separate" principle expressed in formal clothes. "It was just that I didn't see how I could project myself into dressy clothes of any kind," Jeanne says. "They weren't *in* me, I thought. That had always been the one thing I thought I could never do. But of course when I really got started," she adds, "I found doing dressy clothes allowed me as much freedom as sports clothes. I managed to be pretty daring finally—splashed sequins here and there and used all sorts of fancy details."

Returning to the subject of separates, Jeanne says, "they can be just about anything these days. They're more a *way* of dressing than any particular kind of clothes for particular occasions."

The way of dressing which they represent, in the form Jeanne gives them, proved so popular to buyers of the Sportwhirl line that she often found herself forced to carry several items over from season to season. A certain group of clothes would do so well on the summer line, for example, that she would be urged to repeat it in wool for fall, and perhaps to bring it out again the following summer in new color combinations. Within three years' time Jeanne was making a line twice the size of her first one at Sportwhirl, and the firm's business had doubled.

Generally speaking, she points out, each winter's line of cruise clothes is a sort of testing-ground for the next summer's fashions. Cruise clothes—both fortunately and unfortunately, from her point of view—are sold in smaller quantities and at higher prices than clothes designed for summer wear, and therefore they give her the opportunity to try out certain things she is interested in but which must prove themselves before they can be introduced on the summer line.

The subject of price—Sportwhirl is a so-called medium-price house, whose clothes retail from approximately $7.95 to $45.00—brings her to a discussion of textiles. She likes to design fabrics herself, but normally cannot do so because of the cost factor. Sometimes she does work out a pattern or a weave for a wool, in cooperation with a woolen mill's fabric salesmen. This is possible because the mill is willing to let her purchase half a piece of wool—half, that is, of a full piece which normally runs to sixty yards or more.

But when she has worked out a design for a cotton fabric, things are more difficult. Cotton textiles are printed in two ways: by the screen process, or on big machines which reproduce the design by means of large rollers. Cotton fabricators are willing to make up comparatively short lengths of material patterned by the screen method, but naturally sell them at a high price. They lower their price only if they make up the design on a roller machine—and in that case the smallest amount they will sell is the standard printing measuring from 3,000 to 9,000 yards. And it is too risky, of course, to purchase that much material in order to make up a single sample dress for, say, a summer collection, since that dress may prove to be the season's flop—the one dress out of a collection which buyers inexplicably refuse to order.

Jeanne solves this problem as most designers do. If she has designed a cotton textile in which she has great confidence, she orders a small amount of it—at the usual high price—to be printed by the screen method. And she uses this material in her cruise collection. If the fabric is a success, she can then order it in the larger roller-machine printed amount, and at the lower price, for the summer line.

Inspirations for her clothes come to Jeanne from all sorts of places. She makes considerable use of the Industrial Laboratory of the Brooklyn Museum, where thousands of garments, old and new, are available to the student of fashion.

"The Museum is a wonderful place," Jeanne says, echoing the words of almost every other designer in New York. "It has a marvelous library of books on the history of fashion. It has a whole room devoted to current and back issues of fashion periodicals. And of course it has those long racks and those dozens of trunks full of clothes from every time and every country. Everything there is arranged for the designer's convenience. There are private rooms, each equipped with a drawing board. There are dummies available—if you want to drape—and sewing machines. Why, you could make a whole collection right there at the Museum if you wanted to."

But on the whole she thinks she finds most of her ideas in her own daily life. When she is spending a chilly week end in the country, she is constantly trying to figure out what sort of clothes would make her life there easier and more pleasant. She finds special pleasure in devising at-home outfits for winter entertaining, in country or city. The vivid colors and heavy fabrics that seem most suitable to such things are her particular delight.

As a rule she begins each new collection with a handful of sketches. "Then," she says, "I usually have several colors in mind too—colors that I'm eager to use because they offer a definite change from the colors of the previous collection, of which I'm tired by that time."

Once she has a few basic colors selected, she gathers together tiny swatches of fabric until they litter her crowded workroom like overgrown multicolored snowflakes. The studying of these swatches, sorting them, sifting them, arranging and rearranging them in patterns on her worktable, finally results in the choice of a dozen or two that seem to belong together. She mounts this correlated group on a piece of cardboard, to serve as a guide for the serious designing she then settles down to.

One section of a typical Jeanne Campbell color board may hold, for example, a bit of green-and-red-flecked worsted tweed, a green wool jersey, a red wool jersey, silk crepes in both plain colors, patterned textiles in which either red or green predominates, and a group of neutral-shaded fabrics which might combine with any or all of the more strikingly colored ones. Jeanne's final working sketches, for one group of clothes in her next collection, will illustrate the garments she wants to make up in each of those fabrics, or combinations of fabrics.

One of the ways in which she has frequently distinguished herself is in a fresh adaptation of some well-worn or classic fashion. When the American Fashion Critics jury gave Jeanne one of the Coty Awards in 1955—an award bestowed for outstanding contributions to the field of American design —she was particularly cited for her dress-length sheath adapted from the classic cardigan sweater. That particular sheath proved so popular with her customers that Jeanne had to bring it out season after season and in dozens of materials from linen to velvet, including a horizontally striped cotton knit jersey inspired by her husband's knit ties.

A red checked hunting shirt, of the kind worn by genera-tions of deer-stalking woodsmen, went through Jeanne's work-room and emerged as a red-and-white-checked wool shirt surprisingly lined with white crepe and treated as a suit jacket. Classic blazers, in her hands, blossomed into jackets of gold or vivid pink velveteen striped with rows of tiny printed roses. The old-fashioned artist's smock, which Jeanne appreciated for its comfort, but which she thought would be just as com-fortable and considerably prettier if it were shorter, became her "sawed-off" shirt-length smock. And because she liked the flexible ease of a sweater, and decided it would be just as satisfactory in water as on dry land, she designed a ribbed knitted tube that was advertised as "the sweater that goes swimming."

Experimental and ingenious, Jeanne Campbell has proved that a girl can be comfortable and charming and well dressed all at once, in a wardrobe of separates. This is partly because her idea of separates has an elasticity that other designers have eagerly adopted. She once designed a coat dress, for example, which was featured in *Mademoiselle* along with her own explanation of the classification she had given it.

"I call it a separate," she wrote, "because that's the way you're supposed to wear it. Over a dress it's a coat. Under a coat it's a dress. Over a sweater it's a jumper."

But part of Jeanne's success derives from the fact that she is an active, gay, practical person herself, and is somehow able to translate her own attitudes into clothes that other active, gay, practical girls will enjoy.

She has only one word of warning to dispense along with her clothes.

"The separates that are available today," she points out, "are like the enormous selection of frozen foods available in every supermarket. Most of those frozen foods are excellent. But it's so easy to make up a 'good-enough' meal out of them, that sometimes we get lazy and don't put forth any real effort to express individuality in our meals. A dozen women in the same block, for example, may serve chicken, French fried potatoes and peas for dinner on a certain Wednesday night. That's a perfectly good meal, of course, but it doesn't show any one woman's creative culinary ability, or her personal preferences.

"And it's just as easy," she goes on, "to take this same lazy approach to clothes, now that stores are full of separates designed in colors dyed to 'go together.' Sometimes I think girls are content to make up wardrobes that are 'good enough,' but that don't show any individuality at all."

Her own approach to a wardrobe of separates is to think of its components, not as packages of frozen foods, but as architectural units. They can, of course, be slapped together thoughtlessly, to produce an architectural monstrosity. Or they can be put together in slavish imitation of some design that has already spawned a thousand monotonously similar products. Or they can be thoughtfully selected, lovingly studied, and carefully fitted together in such a way that they express the owner's own special and unique quality.

Jeanne Campbell herself, of course, would never consider building that new house she and her writer-editor husband dream of without a lot of careful preliminary planning. She thinks the planning is part of the fun, along with the actual construction and the eventual occupancy of a house that will undoubtedly express the Campbells' own personalities. And the clothes she designs are intended for girls who think, as she does, that the planning and constructing and wearing of a wardrobe ought to be—and can be—equally enjoyable and equally expressive of an individual's own taste and own way of life.

James Galanos

THERE WAS A GOOD DEAL OF EXCITEMENT IN the fashion world when James Galanos of California received the Neiman-Marcus Award and, in that same year 1954, the Coty Award bestowed by the American Fashion Critics Jury. Many people generally alert to fashion news admitted blankly that they had never heard his name until those prizes were announced. His work was unfamiliar to them and so was the young man himself, with his close-cropped hair, his thin taut body and his unlikely air of a bright tough-minded college freshman. But others insisted they were totally unsurprised. They had, they said, "discovered" Galanos some time earlier and had instantly recognized his talents.

Galanos—the accent is on the first syllable—was neither

surprised nor hurt by those who said frankly they had never known of his existence. He was only too aware that they were telling the truth. But he was amused at the number and enthusiasm of his self-styled "discoverers." He thought their memories were faulty.

His own memory, unimpaired by the excitement of simultaneously winning the two chief awards of the fashion industry, could clearly recall the handful of friends who had offered him encouragement and help long before those awards were made. He could recall equally well most of those "discoverers." At one time or another in the past he had presented himself to each of them and with striking unanimity they had rejected the opportunity to discover him on the spot. They had metaphorically shut their doors in his face—doors that now stood suddenly open wide.

"I can't help thinking it's a little funny," Galanos says. The grin that goes with the words makes him look more than ever like an extremely bright, extremely tough-minded freshman.

He was in fact older than he appeared to be when he won those two awards. He was thirty. For more than half his life he had known that he was going to be a designer. And he had always known that he wanted to produce the kind of clothes for which he is now famous—dresses, suits and evening gowns cut from beautiful materials, molded with exquisite simplicity and grace, and finished with the kind of perfection that makes his customers nod smilingly when he tells them that the least expensive Galanos cotton sells for more than a hundred dollars and that others are priced at over three hundred. But for several years the only women who ever appeared in a Galanos dress were the designer's three sisters, and Galanos himself was living for months at a time on the amount of money he now receives for a single "Galanos Original."

His is a success story so crowded with disappointments and discouragements that it seems to lack only a single one of the traditional obstacles common to such tales. He never had to contend with family disapproval of his choice of a career. From the very beginning his parents accepted his decision, and his father helped him financially for far longer than James could comfortably accept such aid.

Gregory Galanos, James's father, came to this country from Greece when he was fourteen. His ambition was to become an artist. He worked days in a restaurant and went to an art school at night. "He's good," his son says of him now. But slowly the ambition was crowded out of Gregory Galanos' life. First there was service with the American Army during World War I. Then, when he was twenty-two, there was the trip back home to his Macedonian village and the return to Philadelphia with a bride and several relatives who needed his help until they, too, could get established in a new land. There was the hard work of building up his own restaurant and the importance of devoting full time to it as his family increased—as two daughters were born, then a son, then another daughter. The elder Galanos continued to paint in his spare time, but he had accepted the fact that he was a restaurant owner rather than the artist he had dreamed of being.

When James was still a baby the family moved to Salem in southern New Jersey. In that small town, and others equally small in the same general area, the boy grew up. He had no access to good libraries or to picture collections. But from the time he was a youngster he knew he wanted to be an artist, and always he had his father's warmest support.

While James was still in grammar school he began his own self-education from the only textbooks available to him—the art and fashion magazines.

"I bought every one I could afford," he says. "Whenever I had thirty-five cents for one of the better ones, that was a big deal."

He cut out pictures and text and pasted them into scrap books. Alongside he pasted some of the sketches he drew himself in every spare minute and on every spare scrap of paper he could find. He was consciously, deliberately, trying to cultivate his eye and his sense of taste.

By the time he was fourteen his artistic ambitions had been clearly channeled: he knew he was going to become a designer.

Two events that occurred while he was still in high school were of the kind to convince any embryonic artist that recognition would come swiftly and easily. A New Jersey department store awarded James a medal in its state-wide art contest. And a *couturier* in Philadelphia—shown a handful of James's sketches by James's uncle, head waiter in the Bellevue Stratford Hotel where the *couturier* was a regular customer—declared decisively that the Galanos boy showed real promise.

With such encouragement it seemed reasonable to James and his family that the boy should head for New York as soon as he was graduated from the twelfth grade. Mr. Galanos offered to pay his son's tuition at an art school. But the particular school they had chosen failed to open that fall, and young Galanos enrolled instead in the Traphagen School of Fashion.

For his first four months there he studied art. Then, impatient to get his hands on actual fabric, he transferred to a course in draping.

At the end of a second four-month period he left.

"I guess I was pretty independent," he says. "Or maybe I should say willful. But I thought I could get ahead faster on my own. My idea was to get a job in a dress house, where I could watch clothes being designed and made and where—I thought—I could learn everything I wanted to know and then start using it."

His teacher in the draping course had recognized his unusual ability and had permitted him to skip over the study of fabric technicalities and to drape immediately. Even the first time he held a pair of shears in his hand he had been completely unafraid to slash into the material. The lack of confidence that troubles so many students at that point was unknown to him. And now he was equally unafraid to ask for a job in the group of towering buildings along Seventh Avenue that forms the center of the American apparel industry.

With his portfolio of sketches under his arm he set out on his rounds from one to another of those skyscrapers, each of which, he confidently believed, housed several dozen potential employers. He soon became familiar with the names listed on the directories in each of those buildings, and with the reception rooms of the companies they represented. He seldom got a glimpse of the showrooms and workrooms beyond.

Manufacturers' receptionists, Galanos found out, were

trained to welcome buyers and fashion magazine representatives. Their attitude toward textile and trimming salesmen
was efficiently brisk. But to job applicants they were frankly
discouraging. Part of their function was to protect their
employers from eager young job-seekers.

"Mr. Smith is in the workroom."

"Mr Smith is with several customers in the showroom."

"Mr. Smith is looking at some fabrics right now."

These were among the numerous and unanswerable reasons
given Galanos as to why he could not possibly see the one
man, or woman, who would have the authority to hire him.
And on the rare occasions when he was granted an interview
he learned and relearned the bitter lesson which so many
young people are taught: that it's impossible to get a job
unless you have experience, and that the only way to obtain
experience is to have a job.

After months of failure Galanos tried to break through
this vicious circle by offering to work without pay, in the
hope of gaining the experience he needed and also for the
satisfaction of being active in his chosen field. But even this
request was refused. It was explained to him that a dress
house was a busy place, wary of letting unknown youngsters
roam at large through its rooms. They were likely to be,
he was told, more trouble than they were worth; their training would demand the time and energy of paid employees
already doing a full day's job.

Unable to claim any actual work experience, Galanos
persistently showed his portfolio of original dress designs to
anybody who would look at them. At heartbreakingly rare
intervals he actually sold a sketch, usually to a house which

had no full-time designer and which habitually made up its line from designs obtained in this way. His first sale was enormously exciting. But it did not lead, as he had hoped, to the offer of a regular job. It didn't even lead to a commitment for the purchase of future sketches.

One manufacturer bought a Galanos design, made it up, and did half a million dollars' worth of business on that single model. He had paid five dollars for the sketch, and he saw no reason to increase the fee when it proved to be a gold mine.

But even in the face of such blows, James Galanos felt a surge of hope every time he sold a sketch. There was actually a certain grim satisfaction, along with a sense of impotent rage, when his designs were stolen. This happened more than once. Galanos would be asked to leave his portfolio so that the sketches could be studied at leisure, and he would agree willingly. Then, when he returned for a verdict, he would be told that none of them was purchasable. In the beginning he accepted this answer at its face value, however much it discouraged him—until, some time later, he began to notice dresses in shop windows that were startlingly familiar to him. The closer he looked the more familiar they appeared. They had undoubtedly been made from his designs and they bore the label of the house where his sketches had been trustfully left.

He had no recourse in such situations except a legal suit which he could not afford and which, in any case, he could probably not have persuaded a lawyer to inaugurate. It would have been too difficult to prove beyond any doubt that a manufactured dress had not been mere coincidence rather than an evidence of literal theft.

"But I was young. I was gullible. I kept hoping somebody would give me a job. So I went on leaving my sketches whenever anybody asked me to," Galanos says. "What else could I do? I was no better off if I didn't leave them."

The recollection of the amount of work which he unwittingly "gave away" is one of the many reasons why he is careful not to speak glibly encouraging words to young people who see his own meteoric rise as a hopeful pattern for their own success.

He feels that there is undoubtedly a more young-minded attitude along Seventh Avenue today than there was in the late 1930's and early 1940's. He believes the Old Guard, as he calls them, have come to realize that the industry needs new blood and that newcomers must be given an opportunity. In his own opinion a designer who has worked for a quarter of a century or so is likely to grow stale, to become repetitious, and ought willingly to step out to make way for fresh ideas and talent. He thinks this opinion is now shared more widely than it was some years ago.

But when young people ask him for advice, which in any case he is reluctant to give because he thinks his own experience is still too limited to make him an authority in the field, he speaks to them honestly about his own history and what it taught him.

"Unless you're so determined to be a designer that nothing else in the world will satisfy you," he tells them, "and unless you're willing to keep at it in spite of every possible discouragement, every heartbreak you can imagine, perhaps you'd better not even hope to get anywhere at all."

He himself spent nearly five full years without a single job. Occasionally he went home for a few weeks, for the sight of a friendly face and a friendly voice. But he was ashamed to be accepting his father's support and always he returned to New York and his wearying rounds once more. In all that time he never succeeded in achieving anything except the sale of a sketch now and then, usually for five dollars, very rarely for as much as ten.

His freshman's grin is a little more sober than usual when he says flatly, "It's not a very easy business to get into."

One of the few places where he felt at home, during those endless lonely months, was the Traphagen School. There a few of the teachers who had come to know him and to have admiration for his ability, did their best to encourage him. After a long series of rebuffs, their confidence was refreshing, and it was good to be able to talk shop occasionally with people who understood the kind of work he wanted to do and believed he was capable of doing it. It was during a visit to the school that he heard about an opening for a young designer willing to go to the West Coast.

Galanos had already thought several times of going to California—although he had no idea how—to seek a job in the design and costume department of one of the film studios. But even if such a thought had never entered his head he would have leaped at the chance when a member of the Traphagen staff asked if he wanted to apply for the job. The man who had asked the school for recommendations was in New York at the time. Galanos went immediately to the hotel address that was given him. There he found himself talking with a busy and successful industrialist and his wife. Galanos liked and trusted them both on sight. They liked him, too, and were impressed with his sketches.

The businessman explained that his wife, who had always

been interested in clothes, wanted to open a small dress house. No definite plans had yet been made. They wanted first to hire a designer. His pay would not be large in the beginning, but it would increase quickly if the business were successful. Then he asked if Galanos would be interested in the job at a starting salary of seventy-five dollars a week.

"Of course they didn't realize," Galanos says, "that even seventy-five dollars was more money than I could imagine right then."

But it was not the salary that chiefly excited him. It was the thought of actually becoming a real designer, entrusted with full authority for the production of a whole collection of clothes. He said yes as soon as he could speak. He could hardly wait to get started. But his future employers, apparently as businesslike as they were friendly, insisted upon contracts drawn up legally for the protection of all parties to the agreement. Three weeks slipped by before Galanos had his own signed contract in his hand. It bound him to work for the new and still nonexistent dress house for a period of five years.

The salary began immediately. But because the business was still unorganized Galanos was asked to remain in New York. More weeks went by. Finally, unable to bear the delay any longer, he begged his new employers to let him go on out to California where he might hasten the establishment of a shop, the hiring of workers, and the arrangement of supply contracts.

In California he met the man who had been hired to serve as the business manager of the new house, and together they did what they could to get things started. But final authority from their backers was still delayed.

At the end of several months they heard at last the explanation of the confusion—and the end of all their hopes: the dress house scheme had been abandoned. The news sounded, to James Galanos, like an announcement of the end of the world.

Once more he started out all over again on the grim search for a job. This time he found one. Jean Louis, head designer at Columbia Studios, took him on as a sketcher. The work gave Galanos no opportunity to express his own ideas, but he stuck to it thankfully, aware that it was a great deal better than nothing.

The industrialist he had met back in New York, however, had not forgotten the serious and talented young man who had been so eager to get to work, and he had not forgotten the five-year contract they had both signed in good faith. So he got in touch with Galanos and offered to send him to college, if further education would be useful to him in lieu of a designing job.

The generous offer was discussed at length. Galanos understood the reasoning behind the proffered scholarship. But he did not want to immerse himself in school again.

"Well, how about a trip to Paris then, to look at the way designers work over there, or a couple of years of travel and study through Europe?" the businessman suggested.

And that was an offer which Galanos had no desire to refuse. He had been sketching at Columbia Studios for seven months when he left for New York and took passage for France.

The logical first step in Paris, he believed, since he knew

no one who could give him entree to the Paris dress houses, was a course of study at the Beaux Arts. He was astounded and delighted when the Beaux Arts director, during an interview before classes began, suggested that an art school course might be less valuable than an apprenticeship with one of the French *couturiers*.

"It was a great relief to hear him say that," Galanos remembers. "Of course it sounded ideal to me. I just hadn't known how to go about landing such a chance."

He still wasn't sure of the proper procedure, especially since his smattering of high-school French was inadequate to the task of explaining himself and what he hoped for. But the French family with whom he had taken a room offered to help him out. His landlady said she would call the designers he was most interested in and discover if at least one of them would grant him the privilege of showing his sketches. Galanos asked her to start with the famous Robert Piguet.

To his great delight Piguet himself offered to interview the young American, and Galanos arrived at the appointed hour with his portfolio. Piguet, who spoke almost as little English as Galanos did French, was extremely kind. He liked the sketches. He said they showed marked individuality. But he also said, regretfully, that he was unable to take on a new apprentice at that particular time. And Galanos, lugging his heavy portfolio homeward again, had to remind himself forcefully that the interview had been a valuable experience in itself, even if it had ended just as he might have suspected it would.

But the very next day a telephone call from the house of Piguet asked Galanos to return there. Piguet's director, at Piguet's own suggestion, was inviting him to spend three months in the establishment as the third of its three young designers. No salary was attached to the job, of course, but Galanos was in France on a student visa and could not have accepted a salary if it had been available. Without any hesitation he signed the contract that was offered to him— the contract customary in French houses, to ensure the loyalty of employees constantly exposed to bribes in return for advance information about a forthcoming collection.

During those three months Galanos and his two fellow designers prepared all the designs for the next Piguet showing. Each day they sat down with the representatives of fabric manufacturers or trimming suppliers and chose the materials they wished to use. They sketched or draped their designs. And they had a daily session with Piguet himself, who presided over their work as master. It was he who presented a theme for expression by his staff, who contributed ideas for amplification, who corrected a line here and a collar there, and finally approved or disapproved each completed model.

When the collection was shown that spring the designs that Galanos had contributed were the ones most enthusiastically purchased by the buyers. They were outstandingly the best sellers of the season. He was asked to sign another three-month contract and he was glad to agree.

By the time that second contract had run out a New York manufacturer had become impressed by the work Galanos was doing, and offered him a job in his Seventh Avenue sportswear house.

Homesick for his family and his own country, eager to be self-supporting at last, and impatient to get started on a career in the United States, Galanos accepted. It felt good to return to New York knowing that he had work waiting for him.

"But the job was a big let-down," Galanos says. "Each season our designs were expected to be about the same as they had been the season before. I wasn't trusted to experiment with some of my own ideas. I was just supposed to turn out more of the clothes that the house had been making for years. The whole situation went against the grain. I couldn't do what I wanted to do. For a designer that kind of a place is a death house. And I—well, I died."

What he actually did, of course, was to resign. And for one whole year afterward he could not find another job. A few possibilities loomed promisingly for a while, but none of them materialized. His training in Paris and his New York experience did not, he was astounded to learn, add up to a total that assured him the chance to work steadily.

"Things looked pretty desperate," he says. "I finally decided that California couldn't be any worse than New York, and that it might be worth while to try out there for a while."

For three months he could find nothing to do on the West Coast either. The film studios did not know him. Galanos himself did not know the manufacturers. And he learned that his special skill—the ability to create a dress distinguished by the precision and elegance for which the French houses are traditionally famous—stirred no interest at all among the few potential employers he managed to interview. They were producers of inexpensive dresses. They could not be persuaded to any enthusiasm for the necessarily expensive models that Galanos wanted to do and felt he could do most effectively.

Jean Louis, for whom he had worked at Columbia Studios, did his best for his former employee. He sent Galanos to various people who might have been expected to appreciate his ability, but still no job offers resulted. Finally Louis made the suggestion and the generous gesture that was to prove a turning point in the young man's life.

"Why don't you," Louis said, "make up a couple of your designs and show the finished dresses to a few of the stores? I know an excellent custom dressmaker, Madame Marguerite —she worked at Hattie Carnegie's at the same time I did, some years ago. I'll ask her to work with you. And I'll put up enough money to finance the first few models."

Galanos accepted the offer with gratitude, but with no very lively hopefulness. Madame Marguerite, however, was willing to cooperate in the enterprise. And not long afterward, with three or four dresses in a box under his arm, Galanos called on the Saks-Fifth Avenue store in Beverly Hills. A New York buyer who happened to be there at the same time took one look at his dresses and left. Galanos understood her point of view and it was fortunate he did because he was to encounter it many times in the next few years. She had obviously admired his dresses, but she knew her customers. If they paid high prices for their clothes it was usually as much for the garments' snob appeal as for their intrinsic beauty. A price tag in three figures should buy them, they thought, not only admiration but the right to brag about the source of a dress.

They were—such women still are—what Galanos himself calls "label conscious," and at that point in his career his own name had no connotation of expensive chic. The purchaser of a Galanos dress would be buying nothing more than a dress, however beautiful it might be. She would have no impressive answer to a friend's "That looks very nice— but whose is it?" So Galanos understood why the New York buyer simply shook her head over his designs.

But the Beverly Hills Saks-Fifth Avenue buyer, in the meantime, was studying them closely. The following day she ordered a dozen. She wanted delivery in two weeks.

Galanos was completely stunned. Unaccustomed to success, the young man had not prepared himself to meet even such a slight evidence of it.

"I ran around all over town," he remembers. "We had to find a place to work—Madame Marguerite's shop was too small. We had to hire a couple of girls and some sewing machines. I didn't know any of the fabric people and yet I had to ask them to let me have merchandise on credit, because the few hundred dollars we had on hand wasn't enough to finance our operation. I had no experience in any of these business matters, but I just tried to use common sense."

Somehow, by frenzied efforts, they filled their first order on time.

Vastly encouraged, Galanos wrote to several buyers for stores in New York and other cities. He had no public relations counselor to phrase the letters for him. Once again he simply used his common sense. He invited them to visit his small shop when they made their next California buying trip, and assured them he would appreciate the kindness he knew such a visit would imply.

The first such letter he mailed out went to the famous Neiman-Marcus store in Dallas, Texas. It was the only one that brought the response he had hoped for. For two months the rest of his letters brought no visitors at all. Even the Los Angeles buying offices, supposedly devoted to a constant exploration of the entire California market on behalf of stores in other parts of the country, did not send representatives to look at his things. But the Neiman-Marcus buyer came.

She too had never heard of Galanos and she knew her Dallas customers were equally unaware of his name. But she studied his meticulously detailed dresses, recognized their special quality, and placed the order that literally transformed the new little company of Galanos Originals from a hairbrained scheme to a going concern. She set James Galanos on the road to success.

"I'll always be grateful to Neiman-Marcus," Galanos says. "It's not only a wonderfully progressive store, alert to everything new that happens anywhere in the industry. It's also unafraid. When it believes in some newcomer it really has the faith to take a chance on him. It doesn't just wait for somebody else to do the pioneering. It realizes that the duty of a good store is to educate a new public for a new product."

Galanos Originals have made fashion history since that first Neiman-Marcus order was placed. But the next two years were still a time of struggle and doubt. Galanos could not afford an elaborate shop. He seated his customers on the few hard chairs he owned, while the sewing machines whirred steadily in the workroom behind him. There were no draperies on the walls. There was seldom a live model on hand to display the dresses. Galanos himself simply brought them out, one by one.

The buyers who slowly found their way to his place seemed

pleased at its contrast to the beautifully decorated salons where most wholesale manufacturers show their collections. But the number of those buyers was still few, and not many were willing to invest in even two or three of the high-priced dresses that appeared so surprisingly out of that small back workroom.

Suddenly a model, who had done occasional work for Galanos in California before she left for New York, reported that she had been wearing her Galanos-designed dresses on Seventh Avenue and that buyers had been inquiring about their source. She suggested that the time had come for him to invade the New York market.

Assuring himself that he wanted to visit the East in any case, Galanos came to New York with a dozen dresses. He established himself in a hotel room, had the dresses pressed, and invited fashion magazine editors and metropolitan buyers to view them. One of his first visitors was a magazine editor who became so enthusiastic over what she saw that she inaugurated a one-woman campaign on their behalf.

"I think she literally dragged some of the buyers up to my show room," Galanos says admiringly. But there was only a handful of them, all told, and although they expressed great admiration for the little collection, they simply did not buy.

They remembered what they had seen, however. The next time Galanos returned to New York—again as much for the pleasure of the visit as with the hope of really impressing the New York buyers—they came to look once more. A few other buyers dropped in, too, people who had not heard about him before. But still nobody bought.

The following season Galanos formally showed his collection in California. Some of the New York buyers, who happened to be in Los Angeles at the time, came to his show out of curiosity. And when he brought that same collection to New York shortly afterward they were intrigued enough to look at his things again.

On that visit Galanos was able to reverse his usual modest habit of displaying his dresses on a hotel room rack. That time he presented his collection in a beautifully decorated apartment that had been lent to him for the occasion.

"It was all very plush," Galanos says, grinning. "The apartment is really wonderful and—well, the whole thing was sort of unusual."

Buyers weary of Seventh Avenue sidewalks flocked to the exclusive address mentioned in the announcement Galanos had sent to the trade journal, *Women's Wear Daily*. The apartment was crowded on the first day of the show.

"And on the second day—before I knew it—I was swamped!" Galanos says. "For the whole ten days I was there, people kept coming all day long."

He takes a deep breath even now, remembering that occasion. The date was 1953. After fifteen years of almost unending struggle he had finally reached his goal. Seventh Avenue wholesale houses were complaining about the money that was being spent on the California designer's clothes instead of on their own. Buyers frankly admitted that they were cutting down their scheduled purchases from established houses to buy at least a few Galanos numbers.

"They just wanted something new, of course," he explains it. "It just happened to be my time. But I had finally hit."

There was no doubt about it. It was an accepted fact.

James Galanos was a success in the town where he had been unable to work, even without pay, not long before.

And it was not an overnight success which died away the next morning. Two years later it was still growing. When *Life* magazine reported the influx of buyers into New York for the fall showings of 1955, it carried a full-page picture of James Galanos displaying his models. The accompanying text said, "Early in the show applause from the spectators broke out spontaneously, swelling until, in an almost unprecedented moment in American dressmaking, the country's hard-boiled fashion pros were on their feet, clapping and cheering."

"I get plenty of job offers now," Galanos adds, when he tells his story. And he grins again. "But I'm not interested. I like running my own business."

At this point he is likely to admit that he is still not certain of the techniques of that process.

"I don't really know much about business," he says. "I've never hired any publicity agents. I still don't know enough about the stores throughout the country, and I've made mistakes because of that—sold my things to shops that don't really have the clientele for them. These matters have to be worked out to everybody's best advantage, and that takes time. Everything takes time. And I don't have many rules to go by. I just try to gain the confidence of the people who work for me, and let myself be guided by conscience and common sense."

For a long time, in the early years of Galanos Originals Incorporated, he worked anywhere from fourteen to eighteen hours a day. A presser in his shop, who insists that Mr.

Galanos is the most wonderful boss in the world, says she never in her life has seen a man work himself so hard. But now, Galanos himself says, he can relax a little—though the speed and energy with which he does everything, the attention he gives to every smallest detail, suggests that what he calls relaxation would be called something else by most people.

"Things are sort of falling into place now," he explains. "I've engaged models. I send out printed announcements when I'm going to have a show. And when I get better organized, and more businesslike, I hope to expand. But the important thing for me to remember is that I've been given my chance. Now it's up to me to maintain my stand- ards—to keep on doing what I'm doing, and to do it better all the time."

He thinks he is one of the luckiest people he knows. He had a long journey to the top, and he remembers every difficult inch of the way. But he does not remember with bitterness or anger.

"After all," he says, "I'm one of the very few designers who can do exactly what he wants. If I choose to use very expensive materials, there's no one to stop me. I don't have to design and make my clothes to fit a certain cost pattern, to be sold at a certain price, as do most designers in the wholesale market. I make the kind of dresses I want to make, and price them when they're finished. And so far it's been all right. The people who buy my things seem to feel they're not being cheated."

His clothes are never startling, though he occasionally likes to be dramatic and he definitely likes to experiment. He thinks the Paris designers are, on the whole, more experimental than Americans, and he thinks this is a quality that should be more emulated here. But he realizes that in France the custom-made dress, the high-priced *couture*, can exist because the economic and social climate is more agreeable to it there. Labor is cheaper in France, for one thing. And customers are more willing to spend long hours in the fitting room while their dressmakers achieve final perfection.

"American women usually lead such active lives that they don't have time for that," Galanos reminds himself.

Cut and detailed finishing are the outstanding characteristics of his own fabulously simple dresses. "He is a master of understatement," another designer says of him admiringly. "He may use a wonderfully intricate cut, and very elaborate workmanship—all those infinitesimal pleats at the waist of a skirt twelve yards around at the bottom!—but the whole effect is invariably quiet. His dresses are *gentle*. They are designed in relation to the women who will be wearing them, not as showy pieces of artistic achievement. When a woman is wearing a Galanos dress, it is always the woman—never the dress itself—that comes into a room first."

"It's an effort for me to put anything *on* a dress," Galanos says. And usually his only trimmings are a fold of the dress material itself, a burst of pleats, the rare sharp contrast of a small white collar on demurely dull black silk, a pair of white cuffs on faintly glistening navy taffeta. He works for "a good shape, a young feeling."

"I'm not afraid to be simple," he says. "I think some people are afraid that if a dress is simple it doesn't look like anything. In design I think it's vitally important to know when to stop."

68

It is only when he is purchasing materials that he himself finds it difficult to know when to stop. They are invariably the most beautiful he can find, whether they are fine domestic cottons or the most delicate of imported silks.

But even on the subject of materials he stands on his own sure ground. "I may be extravagant sometimes," he explains himself, "but I'm—well, how can I put it? I'm not a *crazy* designer."

The people on Seventh Avenue who could not be bothered to interview him a few years ago, are now convinced of that, too.

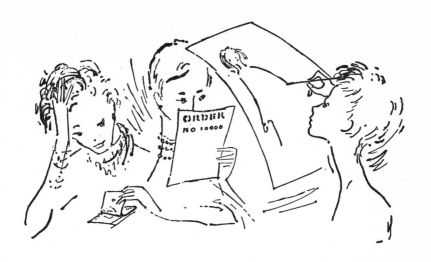

The Frankfurt Sisters of Dallas

THERE WAS A TIME, NOT VERY LONG AGO, when every expectant mother, rich or poor, determinedly chic or frankly dowdy, endured the months of her pregnancy in a depressingly shapeless garment whose hemline invariably sagged at the back and hiked up in an ugly curve at the front to accommodate her bulging figure. She was wearing what was then called a maternity dress, a name that had come to symbolize grim necessity—a kind of hideous navy blue or

71

black sackcloth in which a woman had to do advance penance for the joys of motherhood.

But within less than a decade, following the year 1938, the maternity dress changed its character. Now it is something to be gay in, a dress worn for pleasure as well as for the anticipation of pleasure. Today's expectant mother does not brood at home, reluctant to expose herself to a stranger's eye. She looks pretty and she knows it, and she enjoys herself. If there is truth in the long-held belief that a happy mother-to-be has happy babies, then modern maternity clothes are probably helping immeasurably to produce future generations of cheerful children.

But three of the important founders of this new philosophy in maternity clothes would probably not ever discuss it as solemnly as all that. These young women, who created the Page Boy Company and who own and operate it today, are as lighthearted as the clothes they introduced to a grateful world. In their home town of Dallas, Texas, they have a wonderful time as well as a wonderfully thriving business. They enjoy themselves as much as their customers enjoy their dresses.

Folks in Dallas know perfectly well that there are really only three brown-eyed, brown-haired Frankfurt sisters, but sometimes they feel there must be at least six of them.

There is Elsie, for example, who looks small and pretty and born to dance in tiny-waisted wide-skirted tulle. But Elsie is also E. Frankfurt, president of the Page Boy Company and the first woman ever elected to membership in the Young Presidents' Organization, that group of business executives each of whom, by the age of thirty-nine, has become head of a firm that does at least a million dollars' worth of business annually.

And there is smooth-haired handsome Edna Frankfurt Ravkind, wife of Abe Ravkind, Dallas businessman, and enthusiastic mother of Billy, Sidney and Joan. But she is likewise Miss Edna, vice-president and production manager of Page Boy and competent boss-lady of the hundred and fifty employees in the girls' factory.

Gay attractive young Louise Frankfurt Gartner could not live down the giddy nickname of Toots even when she married the Dallas jeweler, Charles Gartner. Louise plays with her two children every evening—but spends her days in the Page Boy factory workroom, choosing fabrics and designing the company's line, which now includes almost every kind of garment an expectant mother might wish for, from denim shorts and slacks to airy lingerie and formal evening gowns.

The Frankfurt sisters' business is a sort of happy phenomenon that began one hot June afternoon in 1938 when Edna, already married and expecting her second child, stopped at her mother's house for a visit. That was the afternoon Elsie made a remark that has become historic in the family—one of those remarks, half-pitying, half-scornful and wholly self-complacent, which slim young girls have probably made to their child-bearing elder sisters since time began.

"You look horrible," said Elsie to Edna. "Like every other pregnant woman I've ever seen, you look like a beach ball in an unmade bed."

It might have started a family quarrel. Instead it started a lightning-swift chain of events over which bankers and astute statesmen in the world of finance are still blinking dazedly. Edna did not give birth to her son Sidney until some four months later. But that very afternoon, on the porch of the comfortable Frankfurt house, Elsie created the brain-child that would make a fortune for herself and her sisters—and which has helped thousands of expectant mothers face their own frank young sisters with equally frank pride.

But neither Elsie nor Edna knew that anything remarkable was about to happen. Edna, wearing a dress of her mother's, because it was the only thing she could get into, agreed sadly with Elsie's candid appraisal. "But what do you expect?" she murmured. Mrs. Frankfurt placidly reminded her daughters that young mothers-to-be had once looked even worse. Before her own children were born, she said, she had had to wear ungainly Mother Hubbards in which she never dared to go out of doors.

For a moment then it looked as if the talk might settle down to normal family matters—to how young Louise was doing in high school, to Mr. Frankfurt's latest real estate venture, to what sort of a job Elsie was going to look for now that she had just finished college.

That last subject was the real problem of Elsie's life right then. She had studied designing for two years at Southern Methodist University in Dallas, because she had always enjoyed clothes and had thought she wanted to work with them. But she had given it up because, she said, "I found I had more desire than talent." Her only reason for finishing college as a major in the School of Business Administration was that all her life math had been easier for her than anything else. But now that she possessed her degree in accounting she was not at all sure of what she wanted to do with it.

74

On that afternoon, however, Edna's immediate plight was more compelling than Elsie's own future. And suddenly Elsie said, "I believe I could design a dress that would make you look normal."

Edna was still staring at her in utter disbelief when Elsie grabbed her hand and dragged her excitedly indoors.

The Frankfurt sisters do not remember, today, precisely what Edna's reaction was when she saw her young sister cutting away part of the front waistband of a perfectly good skirt—a straight navy blue skirt Edna had been unable to wear for months, but which she hoped to wear again after her baby was born. Then Elsie cut a big oval hole in the skirt itself, extending down several inches below the now non-existent waistband. Finally she replaced the waistband with an adjustable tape, and ran another adjustable tape from it to the bottom edge of the hole.

"There!" Elsie said. "Now try it on."

Edna was astounded at the result. The "window" which Elsie had cut out of the skirt was big enough to accommodate Edna's extra girth below the waistline. And, because the skirt's material did not have to bulge out and over that extra girth, the "window" skirt—as it is now generally called—hung perfectly straight at the hem. The tapes held it snug around her waist, and kept the bottom edge of the window from sagging downward.

A full pleated jacket, flaring from the shoulders, transformed the remodeled skirt into a suit. The jacket was long enough to cover the cut-out portion of the skirt, and Elsie stuck a white organdy bow at its small collar, to focus attention on the neckline.

The first time Edna wore her Elsie-designed suit on a

Dallas shopping trip, women stopped her on the street to ask her where they could get one like it.

It was those wistful questions that startled Elsie into the realization that the solution she had evolved for her sister's clothes problem might also be a solution to her own job quandary. Why couldn't Edna's new maternity dress, that unexpected dividend of Elsie's two years of training in design, become the basis for an enterprise which would also utilize those other two years of business-administration courses? In other words, why not build up a business out of the window-skirt maternity dress?

Elsie does not believe in time-wasting. With characteristic briskness she went straight to a lawyer's office to inquire about obtaining a patent on her inspiration. The lawyer agreed that it was patentable. The process would cost, he said, three hundred dollars.

Three hundred dollars was a lot of money to a Frankfurt girl. But by now Edna was no longer doubtful of her younger sister's ability to make expectant mothers look—and consequently feel—far better than they ever had before. She offered to pool her own savings with Elsie's. Together they possessed exactly five hundred dollars—which meant that they had a balance of two hundred left over after the patent was obtained. It was not an enormous capital with which to start a business.

But it was enough, Elsie and Edna decided. It would buy a lot of material. And the seamstress who sometimes made their own clothes would help them with the sewing.

Elsie looked speculatively at her original model, now Edna's daily uniform. "You like bright colors ordinarily," she said, "just as I do. Why shouldn't you go on wearing them when you're pregnant? Why do maternity clothes have to be dark and drab?"

"They don't," Edna agreed.

That was one point settled. The fabrics the girls chose were in vivid blues, yellows and greens, in soft lavender and subtle terra cotta. And they were of various kinds—cotton broadcloth, sharkskin, covert, poplin and crepe—but in general they were inexpensive. The girls' second important decision had been to sell their dresses at the one price of $22.95.

"Most women," Edna pointed out, "can't afford to buy a whole new wardrobe of high-priced clothes as soon as they find they're going to have a baby."

Another Frankfurt family story, often told along with the beachball-in-an-unmade-bed one, recalls the night in August when nobody in Dallas could sleep because of the heat. That was the night Elsie thought of calling their business the Page Boy Company. The name refers to the trumpeting page who traditionally signaled the birth of an heir in medieval times. And that was also the night—as Elsie learned when she turned on the light and phoned her sister to report her inspiration—that Edna thought of establishing their maternity dress shop in the Medical Arts Building in downtown Dallas. "All the obstetricians have their offices there," Edna explained, in case Elsie hadn't appreciated the significance of her suggestion.

But Elsie appreciated it immediately, just as Edna appreciated the name her sister had coined. Elsie's only question was whether or not the building had a vacancy on its street floor. Edna learned the answer to that the next morning, on a trip to visit her own doctor. By nightfall the girls had signed a lease. Their shop would be ready for occupancy January 1, 1939, at a rent of thirty dollars a month. It would open into the one lobby in all Dallas which most expectant mothers came to know as well as they knew their own back yards.

Young Louise, who had decided to study designing when she entered the University of Illinois that fall, approved of her sisters' curious new project. Mrs. Frankfurt gave her two daughters moral support and advice from the very first. But she was worried about what her husband would say.

Benjamin Frankfurt had once owned a store himself years before, a general store in the town of Cushing, Texas, where he had settled not long after emigrating to this country from Europe as a young man. When he met lively pretty Jennie Bergman at the St. Louis Exposition in 1904, and brought her back to Cushing as his wife, she had helped him behind the counter. They had done so well that they had soon been able to move to Dallas with their baby daughter, Edna, and there Mr. Frankfurt opened a real-estate-investment office. Nevertheless Elsie and Edna agreed with their mother that Mr. Frankfurt might object to his daughters undertaking the same heavy responsibilities he had had to face as a young store owner. They decided to keep their venture a secret from him until it was an established fact.

But their plan did not work out quite the way they had anticipated. During the last frantic pre-opening days—after Edna had had her baby and was back on the job, helping Elsie and her mother put up salmon-colored curtains and

78

arrange the bamboo shop furniture they had bought so inexpensively at the Texas State Fair—they all looked up suddenly to see the amused face of Mr. Frankfurt at the shop door.

His explanation of the visit was prophetic: the new Page Boy Company was not going to be a secret anywhere for much longer. A doctor in the building had asked him what he thought of his daughters' new business, and a curious father had come immediately to see for himself.

Elsie rattled off a slightly nervous account of their past six months' activities.

Her father's verdict at the end of it was not exactly encouraging. "You sound," he said, "like the match salesman who told people he was in the lumber business."

But a few days later, after the shop had actually opened its doors, Elsie and Edna felt rather more like match salesmen suddenly asked to supply lumber enough to build a town. Every Page Boy dress that appeared on the streets of Dallas had the same effect Elsie's original suit had had. Women invariably stopped its owner to inquire where it had been purchased, and then hurried to the spic-and-span little cubicle in the Medical Arts Building to buy one of those trim new maternity dresses for themselves.

By March the Page Boy seamstress needed an assistant, even though Edna took care of buying the fabrics and Elsie directed the cutting. And in May an Atlanta dress buyer, who had seen a Page Boy dress on one of his own customers, wired the query that started the company on its way to nation-wide success.

"Do you wholesale?" the wire asked.

"Certainly," Elsie and Edna wired back, keeping their fingers crossed. Then they hurried out to hire a loft and rent ten sewing machines. Their first big order, for a dozen dresses to be shipped to Atlanta, was in their hands before the sewing machines could be installed.

Mr. Frankfurt conscientiously warned his daughters against the dangers of rapid expansion. He told them to "learn to crawl before you walk."

But Elsie and Edna had already, though perhaps unconsciously, formulated the two rules that would govern their business.

The first rule was not to be afraid. "We don't *want* to crawl," Elsie explained to her father. They had had the courage to open their shop on a meager capital because they believed they had a product that Dallas women would buy. And Dallas women had bought it. Now the Frankfurt sisters were convinced that wholesale merchants also wanted their clothes, and this was all they needed. They were not in the least afraid of the consequences of having ten sewing machines to keep busy.

The second rule was not to be foolishly fearless, not, as Elsie might put it, to run headlong forward until they were exhausted and out of breath. They had not borrowed money, for example, in order to start their enterprise, because they did not think they would feel comfortable if they were in debt. They still wanted to feel comfortable and on their own. Elsie explains their attitude by saying, "We've always enjoyed running our business. But we wouldn't enjoy it if it ran us. We like to live as well as to work."

Their new loft had been chosen not only because it was

available, and therefore they could get right to work filling that Atlanta order, but also because it was cheap. Its rent could be paid out of the profits already made. It would not force them into debt. And the girls, secure in this knowledge, refused to waste time and energy worrying over what they had done.

Things have never stood still for the Page Boy Company. In fact, events moved so quickly that now Elsie and Edna can no longer recall the specific achievements of five years ago, or three years ago. But they will always remember very vividly the incidents of that first summer.

A schoolteacher friend of theirs, traveling to New York for a vacation, took a Page Boy dress with her, wore it into fashionable Best and Company on Fifth Avenue, and asked to see the buyer. Once more that straight-hemmed skirt topped by a flaring jacket sold itself on sight. The Best buyer put in her immediate order for three dozen dresses.

Then that same friend, delighted with her success and the ease with which it had been accomplished, visited the Associated Merchandising Corporation, whose headquarters in New York's wholesale dress district represents the buying interests of many of the nation's biggest department stores. The buyer of that powerful organization was equally enthusiastic. Before Elsie and Edna had recovered from the receipt of the Best order, they were receiving orders from all over the country.

By December of that same year, when Elsie made out the Page Boy books for its first twelve months of business, she learned that their gross sales had totalled a hundred thousand dollars. Even Mr. Frankfurt had to admit that that was pretty fair for an enterprise begun on a five-hundred-dollar investment.

The company's second year, 1940, had its memorable moments, too. Elsie herself went to New York that year and called on fabric manufacturers. They found it difficult to believe that this slight twenty-one-year-old was actually president of anything more serious than a college sorority, but once she started talking business they stopped grinning indulgently at her and started to listen. She convinced them that the Page Boy Company would be a valuable customer, and when she got home she was able to tell Edna that they could stop running to the nearest department store for a dozen yards of this and a dozen yards of that, at retail prices. Now they could purchase their supplies directly from the manufacturers and at a considerable saving.

That year they grossed $120,000 and it was Edna's turn to take a trip. She and Mrs. Frankfurt left for Coronado Beach, California.

Elsie, back home in Dallas, thinking fondly that the vacationers had just about reached their destination and must be settling down for a good rest, was surprised to pick up the ringing phone and hear Edna's voice. She was more surprised by what it said.

"I've found an ideal location for another store," Edna reported briskly. "On Wilshire Boulevard in Los Angeles."

Elsie's immediate reaction pleased her cautious father. She declared that Edna was crazy, and hung up. Mr. Frankfurt nodded his approval. "You girls will be ruined," he said, "if you take a store fifteen hundred miles from your base of operation."

It required another twelve whole hours, and another long-distance phone call—with Mrs. Frankfurt and Edna on one end of the wire and Elsie and her father on the other—before the matter was actually settled and the Los Angeles lease was signed.

Today when businessmen murmur in shocked tones over the speed at which Page Boy has grown, Elsie tells them quite seriously that she and her sisters have never rushed into things. They discuss matters first in great detail, she insists, even to the extent of delaying a decision for fully half a day on occasion.

The next move, however, required no real discussion at all. They took in their youngest sister, Louise. Louise had completed college during the first four years of the company's existence and in 1941—having turned down the offer of a scholarship at a New York fashion school—she started her career in the Los Angeles Page Boy shop. The first dress she produced, when she began to take over the designing end of the business shortly afterward, became famous almost overnight. A motion picture star ordered it right away— ordered a whole wardrobe of it, in every available color. After that almost every Hollywood star who was having a baby became a walking advertisement for Louise's crisp colorful dresses.

The high national birth rate of the years of World War II meant a continued increase in business for Page Boy. By 1946 they realized they had to hire a sales manager, and their choice was vigorous young Bill Moser.

Moser was a little dubious about working for three young women who had, so far, handled every aspect of their own affairs.

"Do you really want me to *manage* the sales?" he asked.

"Of course," Elsie promised him. "From now on you are in complete control." And she meant it.

Delegating authority to good employees, and making sure those employees enjoy what they are doing, is one of the most important planks in the Page Boy president's platform.

"A worker in our shop once said, 'I'm always proud to tell people I'm with Page Boy,'" Elsie recalls. "Of course I was very pleased," she adds, "and I told her so. And then I said—and I meant this too—that if she stopped feeling that way, I hoped she'd leave us. I don't think people ought to be unhappy in their jobs. It's not fair to them, and it's not fair to their employers."

The truth is that Page Boy employees do not leave very often. Maybe this is because the factory the Frankfurt sisters built in 1948 was what Elsie calls "the kind of factory we wanted—not the kind people said we ought to build." It is on the outskirts of Dallas and full of light and air. On the first floor is a retail shop—there is a second one now, too, in the heart of Dallas, replacing the first tiny Page Boy outlet in the Medical Arts Building—and opening off of the shop are the offices of the president, the vice-president and Louise, the secretary. Already this factory is not large enough for the output needed if they accepted all the orders that come in. One of these days, Elsie says, when they can get around to it without feeling rushed and harried, they'll build a new one on the four-acre tract they recently purchased in the heart of Dallas's newest industrial development.

No Page Boy employee ever has to worry that if she does something to please Miss Edna, she may be displeasing Miss Elsie or "Tootsie."

"People are surprised that we get along so well together," Elsie says, sounding surprised herself. Getting along well together seems to all three of them perfectly usual and scarcely worthy of comment. Each has her own sphere, and they do not interfere with each other. But at lunch each day they thresh things out, so that each always knows exactly what is going on in every aspect of the business.

"You eat lunch together every day?" people sometimes inquire in amazement. "Well, of course," the sisters reply matter-of-factly. "Naturally we do." And if they do not have time to go out to lunch, or if the Texas sun is too hot, they are delighted at the excuse to eat in the big gaily decorated, air-conditioned room that serves as headquarters for Elsie and Edna.

It was originally intended as two rooms, that big cheerful office. But Elsie and Edna both chose the same wallpaper, when the building was nearing completion, and so they decided to treat it as a single unit. Their two desks can be isolated from each other by a folding partition—a partition that has yet to be pulled out into place. The Frankfurt sisters simply do not feel any impulse to be shut away from each other.

They are not consciously setting an example, but their attitude of mutual respect and trust and admiration is undoubtedly a factor in the general air of good will throughout the staff. They do things the way they do because it seems natural, just as it seems natural to them to do business without borrowing money.

"A businessman I was talking to the other day," Elsie says, "explained to me that of course he always operates on loans. If he can't get a loan at one bank, he said, he tried another. And I said to him, 'But what would you do if you ran out of banks?' "

This sort of matter-of-fact common sense, which sometimes sounds naive to other industrial experts—until they read the annual profit figures of the Page Boy Company—seems to be the solid core around which the business has been built since its very inception. The day Elsie cut that hole out of her sister's skirt she was simply doing what seemed to her the sensible thing.

"After all," she says, "engineers design *around* obstacles. Why shouldn't clothes designers, too? The Page Boy 'window' skirt doesn't try to conceal or camouflage that perfectly obvious bulge in a pregnant woman's figure. It's designed *around* it."

The art of the magician—which persuades you to watch his right hand while his left is busy deceiving you—is also matter-of-factly utilized to complete a typical Page Boy dress. Striking details near the shoulder line—in the form of gay scarves, collars, bows or embroidery—hold the observer's eye and thus distract attention from the outward-flaring hem of the jacket.

Page Boy dresses—now one of several rival trade-marked groups of dresses manufactured especially for the pregnant figure—run the fashion gamut from the sturdiest cotton to the most elaborate silks and laces. Now they are available in eight Page Boy shops and through more than five hundred other stores. Now they sell for as little as a few dollars each and for as much as a hundred or more. Every year they express the season's newest trends in fabrics and reflect its most popular new colors. But all Page Boy dresses still adhere faithfully to the basic common sense of Elsie's first inspiration.

"Any idea basically sound, with the proper publicity," Elsie once told a group of business girls, "can be built into big business. But the product must be the best of its kind. Don't be afraid. You've got to work. There is no magic. But if you love what you're doing it isn't hard work."

Her sisters would agree with every word she said. They know the idea behind their Page Boy dresses is basically sound. They understand the value of publicity, as they proved with special drama on the occasion when they held a maternity-dress fashion show in New York's exclusive Stork Club. Their customers assure them their product is the best of its kind. And they've never been afraid, either of hard work or of responsibility.

They also insist upon loving the work they do. That's why they won't expand to the point where they themselves become exhausted and unhappy. Perhaps one of the reasons why their clothes have made so many women happy is that the Frankfurt sisters believe in being happy themselves. That, they think, is the only normal, matter-of-fact way of looking at things.

Helen Lee

ASK ANY HUNDRED WOMEN THE QUESTION, "IS there ever a good reason for buying a dress you do not really like?" and probably a good many would answer, "Yes—under certain circumstances." They might buy such a dress, they will tell you, because it was a bargain, because it was obviously fashionable if not so obviously becoming, because it seemed especially practical for commuting, say, or for travel, or because it would be suitable for a certain specific occasion. But ask that question of a hundred wearers of Helen Lee clothes and the answer will invariably be "No!"

Wearers of her clothes are not usually budget-minded. They are not interested in what is fashionable and what is not. Practicality and suitability are words they seldom use.

89

Many of them do not even know whether a dress is becoming or not, and what is more they may not particularly care. To them a dress is a specific object in itself, not an expression of their own personalities or a useful tool for service of self-improvement. They are, in fact, in many ways a very special group. They range in age from 6 months to 14 years. And—except for the youngest of them, who can not yet express their opinions at all—they make it clear that they think it is ridiculous to own dresses they do not like. By their standards the only reason for wearing Helen Lee clothes is because they do like them.

This suggests, perhaps, that Helen Lee's job is an easy one, that all she has to do is find out what very young women like and then supply it to them in large quantities. But the little-girl-who-knows-what-she-likes—in Memphis or Milwaukee, in San Francisco or Syracuse—is not a customer with whom Helen Lee can establish direct contact. She is a customer who can be reached only by way of two intermediaries: her own mother, actual purchaser of the child's clothes, and the store where her mother goes to buy her daughter a new dress.

The mother, of course, has definite ideas of her own on the subject. Whatever her daughter's preference, she is not going to spend money on a dress that seems to her overpriced, dowdy, impractical or unsuitable, or on one that will not wear well and be easy to take care of. And the store, naturally eager to meet all these requirements, adds an additional one of its own. It is not content to stock dresses which will please the chance customer. It wants dresses that actively attract customers, that bring women and children through its doors rather than through the doors of a similar store in the same block.

Helen Lee, then, must do far more than delight the young wearers of her clothes, however important she believes that to be—and she thinks it is more important than anything else. Designing, to her, starts with an idea that can be expressed in terms of fabric, color, line and imagination. But it doesn't end with the dresses she produces out of those ingredients. Those dresses must also form an integrated group which tell a story, which can be advertised so effectively that potential buyers will be persuaded to seek out the store where Helen Lee clothes can be bought. And yet each single dress of that group must deserve the approval of the most discriminating, most fashion-conscious, most sensible mother.

So Helen Lee's job is not easy at all. That she has done it successfully is proved by the fact that a dozen factories now manufacture the dresses that bear her label, *"Youngland" By Helen Lee*. It is also proved, on another level, by the special award given to her in 1953 by the American Fashion Critics Jury, which cited her for "significant influence in the development of good taste and charm in children's fashion." And over and over again, from one end of the country to the other, it is proved every day by the happy wearers of her clothes. When a little girl jumps out of bed in the morning and says, "Today I want to wear my red dress," or "Please may I wear my pocket dress again today?" there is a very good chance that the dress she is so eager to put on was designed by Helen Lee.

Triple-barreled success on those three levels—commercial, critical and popular—does not just happen. It depends on careful long-range planning, as well as on knowledge and talent. The talent, undoubtedly, Helen Lee had from the start. The knowledge she made a point of acquiring. The development of her own kind of long-range plan, which starts with an idea and winds up with nation-wide promotion campaigns that produce multi-million dollar sales—this development is part of the story of Helen Lee's own career.

Helen Lee was born and brought up in Knoxville, Tennessee. There is still a Southern softness in her voice. But when, as a little girl, she talked about becoming a designer that voice must already have had some of the clear firmness it has today. She realized very early that she would never be able to do what she wanted unless she first broke some of the magnolia-scented traditions to which she had been born. During her childhood, in the years just before and just after World War I, Knoxville was still a place where girls were expected to dream only of their first beau, never of their first job.

Looking back as an adult Helen Lee realizes that she felt a small child's natural jealousy of a very beautiful mother. She did not know then that people would some day be writing admiringly of her own brown-eyed, curly brown-haired beauty, and of what more than one reporter has called her pixie-like charm. Like thousands of other children, she was convinced that she could never compete with her mother's looks. She thinks it likely that she first wanted to sew because her mother could not sew at all; here was a field where a small girl had reason to believe she could shine.

She was making doll clothes when she was three, before she was allowed to use a needle. They had to be pinned, each part separately, to the cloth-bodied doll she used as a model. By the time she was eleven she made all her own clothes. Three years later she was sewing for her sister and for her mother, too. By then she was also talking about going away to school to prepare herself for her career. She knew that the one thing she wanted most to do was to make and design clothes.

Helen's lawyer father was more than agreeable to any discussion of college. He had always said that the first step toward a cultivated mind was a broad education, and he applied this principle to girls as well as boys. But once an education had been achieved, he took for granted his daughters would be content with their roles first as charming intelligent debutantes and then as charming intelligent wives. His sons, of course, were duty-bound to build careers for themselves, but no real lady should contemplate such a thing—and Knoxville girls were expected to be ladies.

Helen's mother agreed entirely with this point of view. So did Helen's brothers, one older and one younger than herself, and so did her younger sister. None of them paid any real attention to Helen's repeated claims that she had other and different plans for her life. They simply did not take her seriously. Difficult as it would have been for Helen to fight the well-intentioned arguments of her elders, it was even more difficult to be a persistent rebel when every act of rebellion was met with indulgent amusement. For a long time Helen did not win any of those one-sided arguments, but she never gave up.

After attending boarding school at the Salem Academy in Winston-Salem, N. C., she entered the University of Tennessee in Knoxville. It was not her own choice, because it did not then have a course in designing. But remaining in Knoxville had one advantage over going to one of the famous women's colleges in the North which her parents had recommended. So long as she lived at home she could at least go on arguing for her own point of view.

Finally, at the end of her second year of college, Helen won the permission she had been pleading for. Her parents agreed to let her enter a professional school. Helen left immediately for New York and enrollment in the Traphagen School of Fashion.

The school and the city itself were a revelation to the nineteen-year-old girl from Knoxville. When she first arrived in New York she knew no one, but she made friends quickly and all the people she met took her seriously. It seemed unbelievably wonderful to be able to talk freely about her ideas and her ambitions and to be so quickly understood. Her roommate in the girls' club where she lived—an art student who would soon win recognition as a cartoonist— talked Helen's language. She took for granted that Helen's dreams of a career were perfectly reasonable and sane. So did the other students Helen met at school. It was a heady, exciting experience, but Helen suspects now that the earlier years had their value, too.

"Who's to say," she asks, "that having to face opposition doesn't contribute to a person's growth?"

Of course the most gratifying aspect of her two years at Traphagen, where she eagerly absorbed the techniques of her trade, was the faculty's approval of her work. Helen's designs won prizes, and some of them were sold—at a dollar apiece—through the school's contacts with the wholesale dress industry. The purchased sketches were for little girls' dresses, and the buyer was a manufacturer of children's wear.

When Helen was graduated, and had studied for several months at the Art Students' League, she answered an ad placed in *Women's Wear Daily* by the big successful children's wear manufacturing firm of Joseph Love. The ad called for an "experienced designer." Helen got the job.

"That suggests," she says now, "how little was known about children's designing in those days, how little attention was paid to it. Imagine hiring an inexperienced student as the full-fledged designer for a large company! But the clothes the Joseph Love Company turned out in those days were produced on a hit-or-miss basis, from designs that were picked up here and there. Each season's line was a complete hodgepodge." And Helen was not being asked to bring any order out of that hodgepodge. She was simply expected to keep the large collection moving.

It was taken for granted then, among children's clothing manufacturers, that they served their function if they were ready with racks of variegated dresses when store buyers arrived to make their purchases. And those buyers, who went from one manufacturer's hodgepodge to another, all day long, took for granted that their own job was to pick out from the whole enormous assortment the number of school dresses, party dresses and "best" dresses they could expect to sell in each price range. Their choice was necessarily as random as a manufacturer's purchase of single sketches. There was little reason, except price, for a buyer to favor one company's products over another.

The buyers themselves had no picture in their minds of how little girls might want to look, or ought to look. A child's dress still indicated little but her father's financial status and her mother's degree of pride in keeping a child neat. A little girl's dress was invariably short, no matter what length skirt grownups were wearing. It might be fluffy or it might be plain and practical. But otherwise it had no distinguishing features. A child was not necessarily expected to enjoy wearing it, or to find any personal satisfaction in the way she was dressed. Pleasure in clothes was a joy almost completely reserved for her elders.

Into this rather dreary confusion Helen Lee brought a lively imagination and the determination that something ought to be changed. How to go about making such a change, she did not yet know. But by the end of her four years with the Joseph Love Company she had worked out, in her mind, a rough idea of a plan that would not come to life for some time. She had begun to experiment with the possibility of producing an integrated line, a collection of dresses that had at least some sense of cohesiveness as to style and general approach.

Her next job, with L. Wohl & Company, the manufacturer of Kate Greenaway Frocks, lasted for more than a dozen years. And during that period the name Kate Greenaway began to represent, among buyers, a rather special kind of children's clothes.

The English artist, Kate Greenaway, whose name the company adopted, had revolutionized the art of children's book illustration before her death in 1901. Her quaintly humorous drawings, for a famous edition of *Mother Goose* and for many other books including her own popular *Kate Green-away's Almanacs,* had created in the public mind a kind of ideal little girl. A typical "Kate Greenaway child" wore a big bonnet and a rather long dress, sashed at a high waistline. And though the manufacturer made no literal attempt to copy the artist's style, the company's dresses did have their own distinctive flavor. Helen Lee's style sense was definitely asserting itself, and her work for the Kate Greenaway house helped advance her own development.

"But I still didn't have my own thinking crystallized sufficiently to combat the manufacturer's theory," she says. "You can't argue with success."

World War II occurred while she was still designing for that house, and with it came severe regulations which limited each dress to a certain amount of material. Labor costs and restrictions also contributed to the necessity of turning out clothes that were undeniably skimped in workmanship and fabric. So it was chiefly for the pleasure of exercising her talent a little more widely that Helen Lee did spare-time work during three of the war years for Miss Brogan, well-known for her expensive custom-made children's wear. The experience gained there in matters of careful detail and lovingly expert finishing, proved of permanent value.

After the war Helen worked briefly for Rosenau Brothers, then the country's largest manufacturer of children's dresses. By that time she knew a good deal about producing clothes for the mass market. Now, when she made one of her quick small sketches, she could visualize accurately the whole process that would eventually transform it into thousands of dresses that could be sold at a reasonable profit. She knew the significance, in terms of material and labor costs, of every seam her pencil drew, of every fractional inch of fabric added to a collar or subtracted from a sleeve. She no longer merely dreamed up a charming frock and sketched it on paper. She made, in effect, the blueprints from which profit-earning goods could be constructed in quantity. She had learned her business. Any children's wear manufacturer in the country would have been glad to hire her if she had let it be known that she was willing to leave the biggest company in the industry.

By that time Helen Lee had completed her plan. She thought she knew the kind of clothes that would make little girls happy, not only because several manufacturers had already done well out of her designs, but also because her own three daughters almost invariably gave their cautious approval to the dresses she made for them. She thought she knew how to adapt such clothes to mass-production methods. And she also thought she knew how to sell them to wholesale buyers, and how to promote them so that those buyers would in turn be able to sell them to customers who would enthusiastically come back for more. In other words she had worked out in detail a method for correlating all the steps in the making and selling of children's clothes, so that a little girl and her mother—in Memphis or Milwaukee, in San Francisco or Syracuse—would both be attracted to a specific store and would find there the clothes which would satisfy their separate and different demands.

Usually, however, when she tried to explain this plan to other people in the industry, they did not take her seriously. Once again she was encountering the same problem that she had faced as a girl at home. So when Helen Lee left Rosenau in 1950 it was to ally herself with Sam Landorf Inc., a small company that had been established for less than a year. She had known Sam Landorf himself since he had been a partner of the Joseph Love Company years before. The reason behind her decision was that Landorf understood what she was talking about. Designer and manufacturer spoke the same language. And within a matter of months the dresses labeled *"Youngland" By Helen Lee,* were making clothing history.

There are four Youngland collections a year—spring, summer, winter and fall—and there are from three to four hundred dresses in each one. The fabulous amount of work represented by this output is only part of the labor involved in putting Helen Lee's plan to work. Each of those collections consists of several smaller collections, or groups, and each of those groups can be characterized by a single storytelling phrase that dramatizes their cohesiveness.

"We give buyers a *reason* for choosing our merchandise," Helen Lee says briefly.

The phrase, "A Date with Daddy," for example, would catch a little girl's eye as quickly as it would her mother's. But first it had to arouse the interest of department store buyers, and then of department store merchandise experts unaccustomed to advertising their children's wear from a fashion point of view. It was the merchandisers who, first of all, had to be convinced that a potent ad could be built around that phrase. One of the means by which Youngland convinced them was the illustrations it provided to its customers—in the form of mats ready for newspaper use. Promoting Youngland clothes was thus made as easy as selecting them, in groups, at the Youngland showroom. And suddenly, all over the country, mothers and daughters found themselves attracted by charming illustrations of little girls and their fathers enjoying "A Date for the Movies," "A Date for Dinner," and "A Date to Pose for Portraits." The final phase of Helen Lee's plan fell into place when thousands of mothers and daughters ordered—and re-ordered—those Helen Lee dresses. Their attention had been captured by the lively and imaginative ads, but their continuing admiration for the dresses themselves could only be earned by good design, good quality and good workmanship.

Other Youngland collections have been named and advertised as "Pockets Full of Enchantment" and "Good Enough to Eat." The popular "Wear-Me-With" group was built around a snug-bodiced full-skirted jumper that could be worn with a sprigged and ruffled blouse-slip, a dress-up organdy blouse, a knit tee-shirt, a ruffled pinafore, or simply by itself as a cool trim sun dress. Like many others, that particular group was produced for all age levels, although some Helen Lee designs are limited to the 3 to 6-year-olds, or the 7 to 14-year-olds.

Some Helen Lee groups are promoted all over the country and carried simultaneously by the dozens of stores that sell Youngland dresses. Others are arranged and correlated for a single store, such as Lord & Taylor of New York which four times a year successfully advertises, window displays and sells a special group of Youngland "Little Taylors," each one backed with a fashion idea.

Helen Lee understands the mood of a little girl who wants

to take her new dress to bed with her because she can't bear to let it out of her hands for a single second. The child does not cherish the dress for its becomingness, or for what it "does" for her, but simply because it is, in itself, a delightful possession. That is why Youngland dresses are often in vivid colors, far stronger than the pale pinks and blues to which so many little girls were condemned when Helen Lee first began designing children's clothes. ("Every little girl," Helen Lee says, "should have at least one red dress.") That is why they have wonderful pockets, or wonderful designs of gay recognizable flowers or other identifiable objects. The "dandy lions" that roamed at large over one Helen Lee dress made that garment a private and hilarious zoo to every little girl who owned it.

But Helen Lee knows that at some point every little girl must learn to distinguish between the dresses she loves and the ones that are most suitable and becoming to her. She tries to make this education a painless process by, first of all, offering her young customers clothes which meet both those standards. A child's favorite "Wear-Me-With" dress, for example, with one or another of its accessories, could be suitable for every occasion from school to Sunday-best to birthday-party fete.

Helen Lee does not think it is enough, however, merely to design such clothes, or even to design-and-promote them in such a way that Youngland ads are in themselves a kind of textbook on the well-dressed child. She also travels around the country making personal appearances at juvenile fashion shows staged to introduce one of her new collections.

Juvenile fashion shows, almost unheard of just a few years

ago, are now standard events of the fashion season in many cities. The ones at which Helen Lee is both guest star and commentator are probably the best known and the most popular of all. The adults in the audience invariably react enthusiastically to the small models, as did the highly critical fashion experts when Helen Lee's clothes made their first big-fashion-show appearance in 1953 on the occasion of her receipt of the Coty award. Even the youngest fashion-show guest usually sits fascinated too, eyes round and covetous over the lollypop or ice-cream-cone refreshments served by her department-store host. And on those occasions Helen Lee sometimes slips into her gay running commentary a few words of advice, speaking more as a mother than as a designer.

"Girls who have to wear school uniforms until they are eighteen or so," she points out, "usually explode at that age into a horrible collection of wildly unsuitable, unbecoming clothes. It's not their fault. They've never had the opportunity to choose clothes. They don't know what they want, or why, and sometimes it takes them years to learn. But every mother can help educate her daughter along those lines at a very early age if she wants to take the trouble. Even seven is not too early to begin."

Helen Lee thinks that the example set by a mother herself is of course the most effective form of education. "A mother who takes real pride in her own dress and her own grooming can share that pride with her daughter," she says. But she likes to remind mothers to let girls make their own choices of clothes. "Even if a dress is in poor taste, even if it is really awful," she has advised a mother, "let your daughter have it anyhow if you can afford it. She will learn to improve her taste only by making—and having to wear—her mistakes. And the earlier she makes her mistakes, the better."

The children's wear industry has changed a good deal since young Helen Lee sold her first sketches for a dollar each. She entered a field that was not then being taken seriously by designers because it offered them no opportunity to produce well-thought-out collections expressing a point of view or a personality. It was not then being taken seriously by manufacturers either, who saw it as a business that neither needed nor wanted a strong designer's guiding and influencing hand—it was a business devoted solely to profit-making with no thought of creative production.

She is aware, of course, that the industry is still and will probably always be competitive, and that profits alone will continue to stand as the final proof of success. One incident she recalls with half-horrified amusement is still typical enough even today. She was showing a manufacturer one of her new designs and after an admiring nod he said, referring to a competitor of Helen's company, "That will knock Jim dead!"

"I just stared at him," Helen Lee says. "I wondered what he thought I was making. That little handful of material— what was it supposed to be? A weapon? A sword to slaughter our competitors with?"

But because she knows that designs are always, in one sense, exactly that, she is glad that her own carefully worked out plan for designing-marketing-and-promoting children's clothes has proved financially successful. She knows that if it did not make money it would have to be discarded. But what pleases her most is that designers can now work as creatively in the children's field as in any other. They now, thanks largely to her pioneering efforts—although you have to learn about her influence from other people rather than from her—can function as artists able to command the respect and cooperation of their business partners or their employers.

Helen Lee believes firmly that no designer can work in a vacuum. A designer functions at all, she thinks, only when she functions as an integrated part of her industry and her society. That is why, she asserts, she herself did not become a real designer until her plan was in operation, until she could see her path clearly all the way from a piece of fabric through every process of manufacture and salesmanship to the child for whom the finished dress is bought.

But the designing of each single dress is still, to her, a separate task. No dress can exist as part of the overall production picture unless it exists first as a work of intrinsic value. Helen Lee designs only what she feels will be "right."

"When you suddenly think something is right," she says, trying to explain what she means, "you must ask yourself why you think so, and you must be honest about the answer. If your reason is that you believe it will please your boss, or that it will fit in with a trend somebody else has already started, then you'll know that you were fooling yourself about the 'rightness.' Then your idea is not right in the sense I think it must be, right according to some internal voice that may not speak very clearly, but to which you've always got to listen.

"That internal voice is likely to speak more clearly when you're young," she adds, smiling, "and that's when you're least likely to trust it. Learning to trust your own internal voice is part of the job of becoming a real designer."

Time and again, designing some new and different kind of dress simply because her own internal voice has told her it will be right, she has discovered that her new idea coincided with ideas that other designers have been working on. She remembers once dreaming up a color—"a sort of bottom-of-the-woods color, not really any definite shade at all, that I called wood moss"—and encountering great resistance when she tried to persuade fabric manufacturers to dye material in that shade. And yet, a few months later, at one of the fashion clinics where apparel industry experts exchange confidences on their forthcoming plans—plans which have been closely guarded secrets until that moment—one of the first "secrets" to be exposed was Helen Lee's new color. A group of manufacturers with whom she had had no contact at all had simultaneously hit upon that same shade as the "coming" color for the next season. They called theirs "faun," but otherwise the two were identical.

"Some things are just in the air," she says, "and several designers may pluck them out at the same moment." In her own imagery, the movement of fashion is like the movement of a great wheel. Some designers, she thinks, happen to move with the wheel, to be always "with" the fashion of the moment. Others try to leap on the wheel's rim from time to time, but are not always able to gear their own progress to its motion.

"In a way," Helen Lee says, "the process of designing is simply the process of *moving with* that wheel."

When she hires a new assistant she demands first of all a good technician, and her current crop of four young women are all graduates of professional schools of design. She expects them to be able to cut and make a dress, in any size, from a typically simple but explicit Helen Lee sketch. She watches them as they work, and welcomes their ideas and suggestions. And when a girl has been with her for six months or so, Helen Lee hands her a piece of fabric—perhaps one which she herself has designed, or one of the group she imports each year for her exclusive use—and lets the girl try her hand at actual designing. As early as that an assistant may show that she, like Helen Lee herself, is one of those who is somehow able to move *with* the wheel of fashion.

"Of course when I'm on vacation," Helen Lee says, "they all design all the time. They just go crazy."

Her choice of phrase, and the laugh that goes with it, suggests that she has gathered around herself a group of young women who share her own enthusiasm for delighting little girls, for giving them dresses that they love.

But none of her assistants, and no other youthful designer of the future, will have to struggle to persuade the apparel industry to take children's dresses seriously. That laborious job has already been done by the soft-voiced Southerner whose family once laughed at her "unladylike" determination for a career, but whose home-town paper not long ago triumphantly claimed that a certain designer widely applauded by the fashion critics of the whole country was "Helen Lee, formerly of Knoxville."

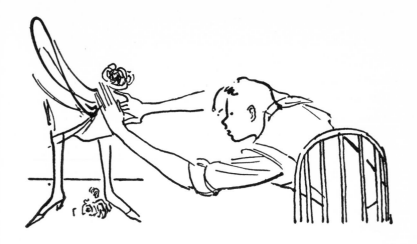

John Moore

AMONG THE SUCCESSFUL IN ANY FIELD WHERE success is notoriously difficult—and those fields certainly include fashion designing—there are invariably a few for whom no obstacles ever seemed to exist. They arrived at the top with such apparent ease and swiftness that less fortunate rivals are likely to attribute their achievement solely to luck. So it is disarming when a young man who, at twenty-five, became the youngest designer ever to receive the coveted Coty Award from the American Fashion Critics Jury, credits his own success to precisely that. "I guess," he says, grinning cheerfully, "I was just born under a lucky sign."

If he is right the sign was hovering over the small town of Wilson, Oklahoma, a birthplace which would seem to lie a most unlucky distance—geographically or by any other standard—from the New York showroom where John Moore now displays his collections. Nevertheless Moore can not even remember a time when he did not intend to become a designer, and he never thought of his home town's location as an obstacle to the goal he had in mind.

John E. Moore, John's father, was a purchasing agent for a group of lumber companies in his native state of Oklahoma when John was born in 1928. Because of the demands of this work the family moved several times, but most of John's early boyhood was spent in Ardmore, a small city in the hills of southern Oklahoma not far from Lake Texoma and the Red River. John remembers the attractiveness and the liveliness of Ardmore with great affection, and when the family moved during his twelfth year he left with regret. The move took them to Alice, Texas, where Mr. Moore established his own lumber yard.

"Of course that part of the move was exciting—that my father was starting his own business," John remembers. "But the country around Alice seemed so flat!"

The elder Moore never tried to persuade his son to join the lumbering business, although he would have been pleased to think of the boy as his future partner. "But what you do with your life is your own business," he always said. And he made only two exceptions to this general laissez-faire policy. The first was his insistence that John attend the Texas Military Institute after his graduation from grammar school.

"He'd always wanted to go there himself," young Moore explains now, "but he hadn't been able to and so of course he wanted me to go." But, again, it never occurred to John that several years at a military school need be regarded as any sort of obstacle to his own eventual career as a designer.

Mrs. Moore, on the other hand—"She's extremely pretty and chic," John says of her—was actively enthusiastic about her son's choice of a profession. She had always been aware of fashion trends and influences herself, and often made her own clothes—a process in which John does not pretend he tried to take any part. "But whenever I saw her patterns scattered around, I always thought they were fascinating," he says. His mother's experimental approach to clothes, the changes and adjustments she invariably made on any pattern she had purchased, gave him an early realization that clothes could be adapted to suit the individual wearer.

Nevertheless Mrs. Moore approved of the idea that John attend the military school, because she thought every boy, and especially an only child such as John was, ought to have the experience of living away from home in order to achieve self-sufficiency. And although—from the scribbled condition of her bridge score pads—she knew John would be perfectly happy if he were allowed to sketch all day, she firmly subjected him to her own special theory of juvenile education.

"She believed that a child ought to be kept busy," John puts it. "It seems to me I used to spend my whole life being picked up at the end of one lesson and dumped off at the next."

He studied piano and practised two hours a day. He studied music appreciation. He took speech classes. He learned tap dancing and is still proud of the prizes he won at student performances. He took lessons in art. Since he had no intention of becoming a serious painter these last probably seemed as irrelevant to what he meant to do as did the other extracurricular activities. But he is glad now for the varied interests to which he was exposed. And the piano, which he continued to study until he was in college, remains his favorite relaxation.

The rigorous program of lessons was reduced somewhat when the family moved, because Alice didn't offer as many opportunities of that sort as Ardmore. But within another two years John was back on another rigorous schedule, at the Texas Military Institute in San Antonio. When, during his junior year, his family moved to the same city—because Mr. Moore closed up his lumber business during World War II in order to work for a government fuel allocation board—John remained a boarding student at the school and under its strict discipline.

Of course John had always hoped to enter a professional design school as soon as he completed his academy training, but this was the point at which his father issued his second and final ultimatum. A general education, Mr. Moore said, was the necessary background for any kind of specialization, and he refused to give his permission for John to go anywhere except to an accredited college.

Young Moore was able to exert his own will only by refusing to enter the University of Texas, where most of his friends were enrolling and where his parents had expected him to go. He remained in San Antonio instead and attended the smaller Trinity University.

"I was certainly never a brilliant student," he says. "But I might have been a better one if I'd applied myself. The trouble was I didn't think any kind of education could be very important unless it was the special kind I wanted. By now, of course," he adds, "I've come to realize how important it is to get a good general education, not just for what it can mean to you professionally but for what it can mean to you as a person."

During his freshman year at Trinity he scribbled fashion sketches all over his notebooks, and took courses in dramatic art as a reluctant second choice to the nonobtainable courses in designing which he would have preferred. The high point of the year, for him, was designing his own costumes—which his mother made—for his appearance in a student production of *The Taming of the Shrew*.

But by the end of that year his stubborn preference for Trinity had worn itself out, and he transferred to the University of Texas. Its only designing courses were given in the school of home economics, however, and so again he chose dramatic arts as his major. And again he appeared, this time in a different role, in *The Taming of the Shrew*.

"I had low grades in everything but dramatics," he says. The applause his stage appearance won gave him his only brief urge to devote his life to some other career than designing. "*The Taming of the Shrew* kind of went to my head that time," he remembers, "and I told my folks I was thinking about going on the stage. Dad said, 'For Pete's sakes! I think you'd have a tough enough time getting anywhere as a designer. I can't believe you'd ever get *any*where on the stage!' " But there was no serious argument on the subject, because John's stage ambitions didn't last long.

The next summer he enrolled in speech and stage costuming courses at Northwestern University. He found Chicago exciting, and attended every play given in the city during July and August. The one he chiefly remembers is *Private Lives*, and the reason he remembers it so well is that Tallulah Bankhead's costumes had been designed by Mainbocher. "I made detailed drawings of every dress she wore," he says.

The summer's other major event was the grade he received for his sketches in the costume design course. "I got an A plus," he recalls. "The professor even wrote 'Excellent!' in the margin."

But back at the University of Texas that fall, with no designing courses to stimulate him, he gave most of his attention to the social life that centered around his fraternity.

"We had some fine parties that fall," he says thoughtfully, "but my grades got even worse."

That winter, during the Christmas vacation, his father finally gave in. "He said to me," John remembers, " 'I suppose you're old enough now to know what you want to do. Go on to New York.' "

But John finished out the year, and spent the following summer as a laborer in his father's lumber yard, now reopened in Alice. He drove a truck, and loaded cement and lumber all day every day. His good-looking fairness burned black, and his school-taught Spanish improved considerably as he worked steadily with the Mexican-born employees on his father's payroll.

"Then at the end of the summer," John says, "I took all the money I'd earned and—this was typical of me—I spent it all on a signet ring which I'd designed myself and had custom made at Tiffany's."

He does not say what his father's reaction was to that

extravagant gesture, but Mr. Moore did not rescind his offer to give John the tuition fee for Parson's School of Design in New York, and an allowance to permit him to live on his own. The elder Moore did suggest, however, that it might be a good idea for John's mother to go East with him, and to see that he got settled in his new life. Mrs. Moore was delighted at the prospect. A native Oklahoman, like her husband, she has always—unlike him—loved New York. She and John packed up the back of the car with their luggage and were ready to start out.

At the last minute John asked his father what route he ought to take. None of the Moores had ever driven eastward before, and he had no idea of the best highways to follow. Mr. Moore admitted that he did not know himself. But— since it was too late to ask for professional advice—he offered his own solution to the problem: he laid out a map of the United States, put one end of a ruler on the town of Alice and the other end on New York, and drew a straight line connecting the two. "That would be the shortest route," he pointed out, half seriously.

"Then that's the one we'll take," John told him. "We certainly can't go far wrong if we follow it."

They did follow it, meticulously, making their way by whatever roads they could find—some of them were scarcely more than lanes—from one town on that ruled line to the next. "I think we were even driving through cow pastures part of the time," John says, grinning.

The gypsy-like journey did bring them eventually to their destination, and they registered at a hotel on Fifty-Seventh Street that had been recommended to them by their only acquaintance in the city, Mrs. Moore's sister-in-law.

"My room was really just a little cubbyhole," John says. "Not that I minded, of course. I thought New York was so exciting that living in a little cubbyhole seemed wonderfully Bohemian. But it was terribly expensive and my allowance wasn't very big. Mother didn't have much money either. I remember a couple of days when we were practically penniless. We still had one of Dad's checks, but we couldn't cash it because we weren't known in the city. Finally we had to wire Dad to get ourselves straightened out. And in the meantime we were eating the cheapest food we could find, at the cheapest delicatessens. But it didn't bother us. We were actually in New York and everything seemed fun."

Mrs. Moore finally moved herself and her son into a smaller hotel where the rates were lower. "It looked awfully tacky. Everything seemed to be falling down," John remembers. "But I just thought, 'This is *really* Bohemian.' Glamorized by New York, that's what I was."

Mrs. Moore's sister-in-law, however, assured her inexperienced relatives that the hotel they were occupying was utterly disreputable, and she saw to it that they moved once more, this time to an apartment in a respectable neighborhood in Jackson Heights, Queens, that borough of New York which lies across the East River from Manhattan.

Not long afterward Mr. Moore came to the city for a brief visit and when he returned to Texas Mrs. Moore went with him. John was on his own.

He was enrolled in the Parsons School by then, and finding his courses just as satisfying as he had always expected they would be. He was working now—working hard. Soon he was advanced into a special class created for those who had had previous training in design. John qualified because of his one course in costume design at Northwestern. But to remain in that class, which was scheduled to complete the usual three-year Parsons course in two years, required application.

Even the hard work seemed to John Moore part of the excitement of the city. His only complaint was that he lived so far away from the center of things. A long subway ride separated Jackson Heights from the glittering theater marquees just off Broadway, from grass-stripped Park Avenue where every stroller was at least potentially a celebrity, and from bustling Seventh Avenue where any distinguished man might, on closer view, prove to be Norman Norell, the American designer most fervently admired by Moore.

But the special brand of luck that had brought John Moore across the country by a ruler-straight course, is not the kind of luck that runs out overnight. Through a friend made by Mrs. Moore while she was in New York he found his way to a home in a New York brownstone owned and partly occupied by the popular pianist, Michael Brown. It was exactly the sort of glorified rooming house every newcomer to New York dreams of discovering. All John's fellow tenants had been selected by their good-natured landlord because they were as young and eager as himself. Together they went to the theater, to recitals, to exhibitions, to parties. And any chance empty evening could always be instantly filled by knocking on adjoining doors and rounding up another Parsons student, a hopeful young actor, and a painter whose days were spent at the Art Students League.

During his hours in the Parsons classrooms John was turning out designs that won his teachers' respect. Some of them even caught the eye of influential visitors to the school. The actress, Martha Wright, then filling a singing engagement, asked him to design two dresses for her—and John was invited to attend her opening night's performance in a restaurant of the St. Regis Hotel. Eleanor Lambert, well-known fashion publicist, began including an occasional John Moore dress, made up from a design he had produced for a school assignment, in the fashion shows and tableaux she frequently arranged for charity benefits and other special purposes.

"I guess I caused a lot of confusion among the guests at those shows," John says, looking completely unrepentant. "They'd be reading down the list of the contributing designers before the show began and they'd see, for example, Ben Reig, Hattie Carnegie, Norman Norell—and then John Moore. 'John Moore?' everybody'd be whispering. 'Who's he?' "

But a good many people did know who he was by the time John finished his two-year course. His circle of friends had widened enormously. His cheerful good manners, his blond good looks, his lively interest in everybody and everything new, made him a popular guest wherever he went. Even outside of New York his name had become known to followers of that fashion-conscious newspaperwoman, Alice Hughes, who mentioned John Moore's ability in several of her columns syndicated to dozens of newspapers.

When Moore left Parsons in the summer of 1950 his parents would have financed the sort of first-trip-to-Europe that most young people hope for as a final touch to their education. But John was too determined to get started in his career to be willing to leave New York just then. As the first step in his efforts to find a job he asked Eleanor Lambert to arrange an appointment for him with Hattie Carnegie.

"Miss Carnegie let me come to see her," John says, "and she gave me what I suppose is her stock interview, number one. She asked me to name the woman I considered the most chic, and to tell her why I thought so. And then she said she didn't have room for any beginners among her staff of designers just then."

For two months after that John Moore tried fruitlessly to find employment. He says it was a discouraging time, but he is aware as he speaks that most young people have to try for far longer than that before they can secure a toe hold in their chosen field.

His stroke of good fortune at the end of that period was to meet—at Michael Brown's wedding—the fashionable and knowledgeable Estrella Rosenblatt, wife of a prominent attorney. When Moore telephoned her the next day and asked her if she would look at his sketches, she agreed. She admired the simple good taste and the talent she saw in them. After his appointment with her John dashed home to tell his mother, then on a brief visit to the city, that the very next day he—John Moore, of Alice, Texas—was going to be discussed at the famous Champillon Restaurant, where Mrs. Rosenblatt would be lunching with Elizabeth Arden.

But the knowledge that his name was being spoken over a notably glamorous table was not the only result of Moore's interview with Estrella Rosenblatt. She telephoned him following that lunch to say that Elizabeth Arden had been impressed by his sketches and was willing to take him on as a designer. "You've got a job," she said, "if a hundred and fifty a week suits you as a salary."

John Moore still thinks it is funny that anybody should doubt the reaction of a recently graduated student, still on an allowance from home, to the offer of a hundred-and-fifty-dollar-a-week job. He also thinks it is funny that he should have leaped straight from design school into one of the few custom salons in the United States. By now he can be equally amused at what happened six weeks later. Elizabeth Arden had assigned him a certain amount of work during his first day on the job, and then she had departed for a month-and-a-half trip to Europe. He had his designs ready when she got back. She studied them carefully, one by one.

"Then she said to me," Moore remembers, " 'Young man, you may have talent. And I may be able to use you some day. But right now all I can tell you is this: you simply don't know enough.' And all I could answer," he adds, "is that I guessed she was right." He was once more among the unemployed.

But Moore's helpful friends did not desert him. Alice Hughes offered to do what she could for the young job-seeker, and Moore told her that the one person he had always most wanted to meet was Norman Norell of the house of Traina-Norell. "I told her that the real ambition of my life was to work with him," Moore remembers. So Alice Hughes arranged for Moore to meet Norell in the garment district restaurant that serves as informal luncheon club for designers and other important men in the dress industry.

"Norell arrived late that day," Moore remembers, "and almost as soon as I'd been introduced to him the other men at our table went back to work. So I had a chance to talk to him. He told me right away that he never uses assistants, but he did say he'd look at my sketches."

Norell too liked the young man's designs. He sent Moore to the well-known fashion editor, Mrs. Carmel Snow, and Mrs. Snow also liked them. Then he sent Moore to Hattie Carnegie.

"She looked at me for a minute," Moore recalls, "and then she said, 'Haven't I seen you somewhere before?' I had to admit I'd already had an interview with her and she remembered it herself finally. She said, 'Well, I admire your tenacity—but I still don't have room for you.'"

Then Norell sent Moore to Jane Derby, who was looking for a new assistant. She studied Moore's sketches, talked to the young man for a while, and then said, "You can start work tomorrow."

In collaboration with another assistant designer, and under the direction of Mrs. Derby herself, John Moore helped produce several collections for this outstanding designer's well-established house. Her standards are high and her clothes are expensive. Moore had an opportunity to express his own already-formulated ideas of simple elegance and quiet well-mannered style.

When he left Jane Derby's, at the end of about a year, it was to make his delayed first trip to Europe. By then he had become friends with his benefactor and mentor, Norman Norell, and the latter obtained entree for him—by letting Moore pose temporarily as his own assistant—to the showings of the major Paris dress houses. Even the sunstroke Moore suffered in Venice, and the food-poisoning that afflicted him in Florence, could not dim the excitement of this first glimpse of the great French designers' work. Then, as now, Moore regarded that work as the greatest stimulating force in the world of fashion. In his opinion only Norell, in this country, displays originality and creative genuis comparable to that of the best French designers. To be shepherded by Norell from one famous Parisian couture house to another seemed—to the young man born in Wilson, Oklahoma—like living some wonderful dream.

But when Moore returned to New York he was once more in need of a job. Norell suggested that the fabric manufacturers were often a good source of information on dress houses seeking new talent, and he asked Tom Maginnis of Fortsmann Woolens to explore the possibilities of an opening for Moore.

Maginnis, talking to Mrs. Mattie Talmack shortly thereafter, tried to tell her about the young designer of whom Norell thought so highly. But brisk decisive Mrs. Talmack, recently back from France herself, preferred to talk about something else. She wanted to tell Maginnis about a young man she had noticed among the audience at several Paris collections. "Every time a model was shown that I particularly liked myself," she said, "he seemed to be liking it just as well. I'd be interested in hiring a young man like that. But unfortunately he seemed to be Norell's assistant, and of course I wouldn't consider trying to hire him away from any other house."

Maginnis was finally able to convince her that the young

man she had seen was the very young man he himself was trying to tell her about—and that John Moore was no longer, even unofficially, an assistant to Norman Norell.

It was in 1951 that John Moore went to work for Talmack Incorporated. Two years later he and the house jointly won the Coty Award.

"While he follows the current trends," the New York *Times* fashion expert, Virginia Pope, wrote of him not long after that event, "he gives them individuality. There is about them a youthful flair suitable to women of all ages. Though they are ready-to-wear, the designer gives the clothes he makes a couture touch."

That individual flair which made John Moore, at twenty-five, one of the outstanding designers in the country, is usually most apparent in the silhouette. Silhouette, in fact, is the focal point of his own approach to clothes. The research he does at the costume collection of the Metropolitan Museum of Art, when he is preparing to tackle each new collection, always results in a batch of sketches illustrating various details which have caught his interest, but in most cases the lines he draws are lines suggesting a silhouette. These random sketches serve as the basis for his first finished designs.

"The hardest part of each collection is always the job of getting started," he says. When he brings his first few sketches into the workroom he and his assistant, Jeanne Cateura, drape the designs in muslin. Sometimes Miss Jeanne —or his tailoring assistant, Angelo Madjorov—can work directly from his casual sketch and its scrawled marginal notes. Sometimes he finds it quicker and easier to illustrate directly in the cloth just what it is he has in mind.

"Of course sometimes I've sketched an idea that simply doesn't work out in fabric," he says. But Miss Jeanne matter-of-factly refuses to recognize the apologetic note in this statement. "Of course," she agrees, from behind one of the muslin-shrouded figures that people their workroom like an assemblage of headless ghosts, "every idea doesn't work out. That's part of designing."

Once the muslin is pinned and sewed into shape, Moore translates it in his mind into various fabrics until he decides on the particular one which will most fully express the design's potential qualities. Novelty fabrics seldom interest him. Usually he uses "the basic fabrics that are at hand."

His trimming is almost always scanty and simple, and there are no extraneous details. An exception to this rule may occur, however, when he repeats on the back of a dress the pair of bows, for example, which serve a functional purpose at its front closing.

"Roz Ames, the girl who models for us—we fit most of our clothes on her—sometimes asks me why I've done that," Moore says. "She reminds me that I'm always saying there's no point to things that don't work—to buttons that don't button, or bows that don't tie anything. And she wants to know why I've got bows on the back, where there's nothing for them to tie. I just have to tell her, 'That's one of those things.' I can't explain it any better than that. But I can't seem to put something *just* on the front of a dress. If I start something on the front I like to carry it around to the back, too. Otherwise the dress looks skimped to me—cheated, I might say."

He has made as many as six collections in a single year: a collection of cotton and silk resort clothes, for early winter; an advance spring collection; a spring collection; a summer collection; a fall collection; and a small group of winter holiday dance dresses. Some of those groups include as many as fifty individual numbers, ranging from informal daytime suits and dresses in cotton, wool or silk, through afternoon dresses to formal evening wear. Among the most numerous types in each group are the ensembles—usually dresses and matching jackets—for which the house of Talmack has long been especially noted.

"It's a lot of work," Moore says, "and when you start a new collection you sometimes wonder where the ideas are going to come from."

For him the fall collection is the most important one of the year. "This," he says, "is the time when you make any real silhouette change—when you project the new ideas." And although his own ideas have come from "almost any place, from out of the air," he says frankly that they are always rooted in the seasonal fashion trend inspired by Paris, which he now visits every summer.

"I don't see how anybody can deny the influence of the Paris designers," he says. "It's not that we haven't got plenty of designing talent here. I think we have. But here it's not given the help it's given in France. There the designer is constantly being 'fed'—by the fabric houses, for example, which *give* their best offerings to a designer each season, in the hope that the designer will try them out. Here we have to buy every yard of goods we use. The fact of having to pay for it doesn't make the real difference, of course. The difference is more in the position designers occupy in the two countries. I suppose it all comes down to the fact that designing there is taken seriously as an art. Here it's just part of an industry—a profit-seeking industry."

Miss Jeanne agrees with him when he says, "You can't buck the Paris trend. You have to accept it and add to it what you can give yourself."

She reminds him further that American designers have sometimes tried to offer a completely new silhouette, only to have it rejected by the buyers. "But when Paris 'invents' that same silhouette a year later," she adds, "the buyers are all eager to accept it."

John Moore's final word on the subject, however, is a hopeful one. "The buyers here have finally come to accept Norell's original designs. It took time, but now his position is as authoritative as that of any Paris designer. So it can happen. And I'd like to think that some day I might be respected in the way he is."

Already he has won a reputation for producing clothes that have that "original flair" Virginia Pope spoke of—and of being able to produce them in a retail-price range that starts at less than fifty dollars. It is the boast of the Talmack house that the wearers of its clothes are women of unlimited fashion sense if limited financial means. And it is John Moore's belief that a woman wearing a Talmack dress can appear alongside a friend whose dress has been custom-made, and that the wearer of the Talmack dress will not "feel like an orphan child."

But John Moore will not let either the influence of Paris

or his own desire to design original dresses lead him into producing clothes which, in his opinion, do not fit the times and the occasions of the American woman's way of life. "Clothes have to be able to go places," he says.

That is the principle he keeps in mind when he draws his sketches and does his draping. He is not disturbed over the fact that his sketching skill is short of perfection. "Lots of students get excited," he says, "when someone tells them they do beautiful sketches. But if that's all those students *can* do, they're not likely to be real designers—though they may make good fashion sketches for the magazines." He thinks it is more important that he has learned to drape, so that less and less often now he turns out one of those sketches that "doesn't work out in fabric." When he drapes a new design he is thinking constantly of whether it will be the kind of a dress that will be comfortable and wearable on the kind of occasions for which it is intended.

His own preference is for the gentle afternoon dress, in wool or crepe, "that makes a woman look like a lady—you know, not tough, not hard-boiled." Asked to define the ideal wearer of his clothes he thought she would be "feminine and chic at the same time." And then, asked to define chic, he first grinned and said to Miss Jeanne, "I'd better not admit we always say, 'Chic—phooey!' Seriously, though," he added, "I'm not sure I can put it into words—it's such an intangible thing, a sort of extra sense that some women seem to have. It's the woman plus the costume plus every accessory plus the occasion plus—and most important—the manner in which she wears her clothes."

125

And then, after further thought, he wrote out four very specific hints which in his opinion would help any woman to approach the quality of chic:

1. Simple clothes with no extraneous details.
2. Immaculately fresh white cotton gloves in the daytime.
3. Well-cared for and highly polished shoes, straight stocking seams.
4. The Scrubbed Look, no careless make-up and every hair in place.

John Moore's deliberate self-questioning slowness when he answers a question stands in clear contrast to the apparently unquestioning swiftness with which he has moved ahead in his profession. "If I'd ever drawn a chart of how I wanted my career to work out," he says, "I'd have drawn it—well, exactly the way it's happened."

He is aware of the fact that he was already functioning as a designer at the age when most young people are struggling for their first opportunity to show what they can do. But there is more gratitude than pride in his voice when he speaks of having won the Fashion Critics approval and the Coty Award. He will admit proudly that it was the most important event of his life to date, but he does not speak as if it had invested him with a halo of authority beneath which he can relax for the rest of his life. For one thing, he has no desire to relax.

He is still as "glamorized" by New York as he was the day he arrived along that ruler-straight line from Alice. He is as eager to meet new people now as he was in the days when each new friend might conceivably help him on his way. He anticipates each new play with as much excitement as he did when he had to squeeze the price of a ticket out of a slender allowance. He buys albums of records every time he passes a record shop. And, now that he can afford it, he spends his Saturday afternoons at auction galleries buying antique furniture for his apartment which he says is "not exactly a penthouse—but it *is* on the top floor."

He laughs at Miss Jeanne when she says, "You might better be spending those afternoons in a nice cheap movie, with maybe a cup of coffee afterward," but he proved to her that his hobbies need not always be expensive by learning to cook the cheese souffle for which she gave him the recipe. And though he bragged to her of his success, he meekly agreed that one dish did not make a good cook, and that he ought to try another recipe, too. The one she decided to give him, after thinking it over carefully, was for "a good beef stew, with plenty of carrots and onions."

"I never can understand it when people say they have nothing to do," John Moore says. "I don't ever remember being at a loss to know what to do with myself. I was always *doing.*"

Maybe, he thinks, this is because he was always "kept busy" as a child. And maybe—though he does not say so—this fortunate habit of "always doing" had almost as much to do with his successful career as that "lucky sign" under which he says he must have been born.

Bonnie Cashin

WHEN BONNIE CASHIN WAS A YOUNG GIRL SHE
cut out and pasted over her desk a drawing of two trapeze
artists swinging through the air in an intricate turn, above
a caption that read, "You've got to know when to let go."
She thought then, and she still thinks today, that this was
wonderfully wise advice, and she has followed it in more
ways than one. She hopes it has taught her, for example, to
"let go" of a design when her creative mind has worked
on it to the point where anything further would be superfluous
—would be pointless diddling. She knows it has helped her
to "let go" of a job whenever she felt she had given it her
best, had learned all it had to teach her, and that she ought
to be moving on to a new field.

YOUNG FACES IN FASHION

The last time Bonnie Cashin let go of a job it was to move into a particularly challenging field: she offered her services as a designer to the apparel industry as a whole, much as an industrial designer makes himself available to all manufacturers who need his particular talents. Unlike most designers, in other words, she does not prepare a line or a group of collections for any one manufacturing house; instead she designs clothes of all kinds—for wear from morning to night—to be made up by various manufacturers who necessarily work within their own medium (lingerie, for example, or suits and coats) and within their own established price range.

For Bonnie herself this means the opportunity to work toward complete wardrobes for the kind of customer who appeals to her most—a woman much like herself, busy and active, and alert always to the demands and privileges of her own time.

This "plan" of Bonnie's, as she calls it, is still in its early stages, but Bonnie Cashin is not the only one who has high hopes of what it may accomplish. The entire apparel industry is watching her experiment with curiosity, fairly certain that if anyone can make it work—can successfully change traditional industry patterns—it will be this unusual and outstanding American designer. It would not be the first time that she had tried and succeeded at something new. And on each occasion in the past when Bonnie has let go of one kind of work and gone into a new one, she has brought with her a stimulating breath of the freedom that seems to be her own personal climate.

Bonnie's native climate, literally speaking, is California.

She was born in Oakland, spent her early years in several towns in the northern part of the state, and then moved south to Los Angeles. So the impulses which frequently take her off today on trips halfway round the globe seem to her the natural result of having belonged to a nomadic family. Her inventive father liked to be on the move. Her practical mother could manage her family anywhere—and usually manage a custom dress shop as well. And Bonnie's younger brother showed an early and lasting interest in geology, that profession which so many born nomads find appealing.

But wherever the family lived, whatever school Bonnie attended, one aspect of her life was constant. "I grew up sewing," she says. "My first playthings were scraps from my mother's shop." And she is strongly aware of the advantages to any embryonic designer of having a mother who is a skilled and creative maker of clothes. The first designs Bonnie drew—she says "I think with a pencil in my hand"—were made up for her by her mother while Bonnie was still too young to translate them into fabric herself. "Mother still does that for me today," Bonnie admits, "when I don't have time myself to make up all the things I want to try out. It sounds as if I exploit her, I'm afraid, but the truth is we've always been very good friends."

But clothes were by no means the only interest in her childhood. She read omniverously and especially loved fairy tales, and she feels today that her reading helped to develop the kind of imagination which must be every designer's stock-in-trade. She loved music, rhythm and color, and therefore loved the art of ballet in which all those three elements are intimately combined. Her first job gave expression to the fascination that art form held for her.

Bonnie was still in high school at the time. She did not really need a job that summer—had, in fact, every intention of spending part of it with friends on the island of Catalina. But she knew that her shyness was going to make it difficult for her to apply for work the following year, when she would need it. She therefore decided, after the close of school in June, to do some practice job-seeking in order to learn how to accept rebuffs serenely. Her mother drove her into Los Angeles from the suburb where the family lived at the time, and Bonnie presented herself and a book of her sketches to the director of a local ballet troop. "Would you like to hire a designer?" she asked.

The man looked at her—Bonnie is small, dark-haired, very bright eyed—and looked at her sketches. "Yes," he said, "I would. We need someone right now and I think you'll do. You can start immediately."

Bonnie had been braced for a refusal. She was totally unprepared for its opposite. Startled out of her shyness she protested, "But I can't!" The recollection of her words amuses her to this day. "I haven't had my vacation yet!"

But the unorthodox employer who had decided to take a chance on this very young girl was not put off by her surprising answer. He solemnly assured her that she would be free to take two weeks off if she would first prepare the sketches required for certain costumes he needed without delay. He added that he would give her a retainer to secure her services as designer to the dance troop.

Engulfed in shyness again, Bonnie did not even inquire the amount of the fee. She simply went to work.

Designing ballet costumes, Bonnie thought, was pure

pleasure. They gave full scope to her delight in color, and she enjoyed creating dresses that seemed to move with a rhythm of their own, as if they were part of the choreography. The sketches she made reflected her own joy in what she was doing.

By the time Bonnie was ready to leave for her promised vacation her employer realized that his quick decision had been a wise one. But he was amused once more by his new designer when he learned that she had not asked for her fee—did not even know how much it was to be. "I was afraid to bring it up," Bonnie admitted when he questioned her on the subject. And when he gave her her first twenty-five dollars she felt not only superbly rich but honestly incredulous that payment in actual cash should be given for the fun she had been having.

When she finished school she was glad to go on with work for the ballet company, and she looks back on it now as the real beginning of her education.

In the meantime the productions by the Los Angeles dancers had caught the attention of the owner of the Roxy Theater in New York, who offered to the troop's manager the job of managing that famous theater. When Jack Partington accepted, and prepared to leave for the East, he asked Bonnie if she would like to join his New York staff as costume designer.

Bonnie's first reaction was to shake her head. "I can't bear to think of living in that city," she told him, with what she now refers to as typical California provincialism. "Of course I've eaten those words a thousand times since," she says. "Now I love New York—love living here."

But she wasn't afraid of the job itself, and Partington persuaded her to accept it. It was 1936, and Bonnie Cashin was still less than twenty years old, when she arrived in the eastern metropolis that she now thinks of as her home.

Variety, the theatrical daily, fed her self-confidence with a story heralding her as "the youngest designer ever to hit Broadway."

"There's no doubt about it," Bonnie says. "I thought I was pretty smart."

But her job at the Roxy proved to be of confidence-destroying proportions: she was responsible for the design and production of three complete sets of costumes every week for the tweny-four girls who made up the famous Roxy chorus known as the Rockettes.

"I discovered very quickly how much I had to learn," Bonnie admits. "And I'll always think of my five years at the Roxy as my real formal schooling in design."

She can be very specific about the lessons she absorbed during that rigorous training period. Four of them particularly stand out in her mind now, when she looks back.

She learned, first, to make quick decisions and to work rapidly and efficiently. Her staff of some seven or eight women was competent and devoted. "They all had a wonderful team spirit," Bonnie Cashin recalls, "or we'd never have finished a single thing in time." But despite the quality of her assistance those seventy-two costumes could never have been completed each week if the young designer herself had not been able to think out her designs and plan their execution at top speed.

She learned, second, to develop a sense of resource within herself. "I had a minute budget," she recalls, "and everything had to be done with the strictest economy. But everything also had to look finished and effective." She discovered how to paint muslin—how to "weave" textures with a paint brush—so that that cheap material was apparently transformed into a score of different and far more expensive fabrics. She created costumes out of curious odds and ends that had probably never been employed for that purpose before. One achievement she remembers was the two dozen dresses she made by forming two dozen big circles out of bamboo, and using them to stiffen the hems of bias-cut skirts that curved down and out from the dancers' waists like inverted morning glories. It took all night to finish those costumes in time. Her staff worked until long after the dinner hour, and after their exhausted departure Bonnie phoned her mother—who was with her in New York at the time—and Mrs. Cashin came down to the theater to work with her daughter until dawn.

But the dresses were worth all the effort Bonnie had put into them. Because the bamboo was flexible, and because the material was cut on the bias, the skirts could be manipulated in a dozen ways that had never been possible with dancers' costumes before. The producer, Gae Foster, was delighted.

"I saw costumes made that same way in a television musical just the other day," Bonnie says, "and I've seen similar ones several times on the stage in the past few years. They've become a standard item in the dance wardrobe. But they'd never been done until we did them that night, and they caused quite a lot of excitement when the girls first performed in them."

Those costumes are now recognizable as an early example of the Cashin ingenuity and the Cashin flair for designing something that gives rise to a multitude of copies. But Bonnie Cashin herself recalls them chiefly as an example of how she was learning to use her imagination to eke out limited funds, to find that "sense of resource" within herself which she feels every creative designer must possess.

The third thing she believes the Roxy job taught her was the effect of light on color. "I used to think red was red, and that that was all there was to it," she explains. "But producing dresses that would be affected by stage lighting taught me that red can be a dozen shades. Of course every painter knows this. I paint myself now and perhaps I could have learned it through painting. But I learned it then, early, and it was a valuable lesson."

And the fourth lesson she learned at the same time was the simple but too often ignored fact that, as she puts it, "Bodies move."

"In the Edwardian age," she explains, "women posed in attitudes. If they looked well standing perfectly still, they could be pleased with the effect they created. But our 'attitudes' today are moving ones. We're always on the go, working or having fun. That's why we're so often disappointed when we see a dress pictured in an ad, rush to the store to buy it—and find we look terrible when we put it on and walk across the room: it wasn't designed to be *moved* in. All clothes should be, of course. And designing clothes for dancers was a good way to learn how to do that."

Three costumes a week, for fifty-two weeks a year, add up to a considerable number, and five years of that kind of production gives any designer a considerable amount of experience. By the time Bonnie had been at the Roxy that long she was beginning to feel that she was no longer learning as rapidly as she had in the beginning. Even a job as exacting as hers, she had discovered, could become routine eventually. "I could feel that I was getting stale," she says. "I was beginning to have that boxed-in feeling that every job gives me after I've learned to do it as well as I can, when I no longer feel I'm growing in my work."

Gae Foster, who had good reason to be aware of Bonnie's inventive skill, encouraged her to think that she could be equally successful in some other area of design. And Bonnie herself had confidence in her ability to go on to something else. Her difficulty was that she did not know the direction in which she wanted to strike out: she did not know where she would land if she let go.

She remembered a talk she had had, soon after her arrival in New York, with a woman executive in the apparel industry. Bonnie, "very starry eyed," as she recalls herself, had said, "I want to design the most beautiful clothes in the world—evening clothes, wonderful coats, country things—everything I myself want to wear and own. And then, just for fun, I'd love to do the most fabulous ballet in the world; and maybe I'd do a picture, too, and dress the heroine as no heroine had ever been dressed before."

The older woman had tried to conceal her amusement at this all-encompassing ambition, and had firmly advised Bonnie to specialize. "Be a sports wear designer," she had said, "*or* a dressy designer, *or* a theater designer. You'll never succeed if you don't specialize."

Bonnie, however, had no intention of specializing, except—as she was later to understand more clearly—in what she calls "my kind of a girl, living in a certain kind of way. I felt I'd only be part of a designer if I designed only part of her wardrobe," she adds. And even then she felt, as she still does, that, "If I was also inspired to do theater fantasies—what was wrong, if I did them well?"

But there was, of course, no one job in the world which would permit Bonnie to design all the many varieties of clothes that interested her.

While she was still trying to make up her mind as to her next step, in view of the advice she had received, she expressed her increasing restlessness by designing a complete assortment of regular street clothes for the Rockettes to wear in a fashion-show number. The stage was set with a huge facsimile of one of the top fashion magazines, and the dancing models stepped one by one from between its giant-sized pages. The magazine's editor was enormously impressed by the show. She was surprised that a girl who had already been classified as a creator of stage costumes could turn out garments worthy of a gifted *couture* designer. She, too, urged Bonnie Cashin to try her wings as a designer of off-stage clothes. So did several of Bonnie's friends, for whom she had designed personal wardrobes, or who had admired her own Cashin-designed clothes.

Louis Adler, of the well-known sportswear house of Adler & Adler, was more concrete in his encouragement. He offered Bonnie a job.

"I didn't really know whether I wanted it or not," Bonnie admits. "The profit-conscious, businesslike atmosphere of

Seventh Avenue wholesale firms seemed very different to me from the atmosphere around the theater. I felt more at home with dancers, actors, artists, musicians, writers—people like that—than I did with most of the businessmen I'd met in the clothing industry. I didn't know whether I'd be happy as a part of that industry. And it's always been important to me to work with people who seem harmonious to me as human beings."

Mr. Adler was understanding—and pretty determined to hire Bonnie one way or the other. He suggested that she design a collection for him on a part-time basis, while she still held her theater job. And that is what Bonnie did. Days that had already been full to the brim were crowded even further. But she finished her collection in time.

The showing of Adler & Adler's first group of Cashin designs was an instant success. Bonnie decided to take the step she had been reluctant about earlier. She left the Roxy and made her formal debut into the world of the wholesale apparel industry.

Despite the enthusiastic response to that first collection she was soon encountering a kind of criticism which amazed her. It did not come from her customers. She never ventured into the showroom and never met her buyers at all. They did not even know the name of the Adler & Adler designer who worked—as she had in the theater—strictly behind the scenes. The criticism of Bonnie's designs came from the salesmen whose job it was to present them in the showroom. It was they who complained, and their complaint was that her clothes were "too daring, too radical."

"Everything I did seemed perfectly ordinary to me," Bonnie

says. "For example, I had some jersey and some crepe dyed the same color, and combined them in a dress. It was the kind of thing I'd done a hundred times with stage costumes. And of course today it doesn't sound surprising at all when combinations of dyed-to-match materials are commonplace. But then it was considered radical! Sounds silly, doesn't it? I also inserted a waistband in some of my dresses—another thing that seemed ordinary to me then and certainly seems ordinary to everybody now. I'd learned the value of a waistband when I was making costumes, of course: it wasn't feasible to sew a very full tarlatan skirt, say, to a thin bodice, so of course we'd always used a waistband in between. But when I did the same thing with dresses—for the same logical reason—the salesmen told me it wouldn't sell because it was too unusual!"

The buyers themselves, however, continued to show enthusiasm for most of Bonnie's things that reached the showroom. She points out now that the success of her collections was owing partly to the fact that those early years of the 1940s were in general a time when sports clothes were winning new and wider recognition. But the recognition of her own particular brand of sports clothes was considerably above the average, and Bonnie Cashin's name began to be whispered throughout the trade even though it still did not appear officially on a label.

One of the first proofs of her growing recognition, so far as Bonnie herself was concerned, was her appointment to Mayor Fiorello LaGuardia's committee organized during the early days of the war to urge more volunteers to join the women's branches of the armed services.

"Working on that committee was exciting," Bonnie says.

"We were designing new uniforms and we had to make up our samples with great secrecy. And it was interesting to have an outside job to do when the whole industry was feeling cramped from the wartime restrictions on the amount of material and trim that could be used for any one garment."

Ever since her arrival in New York, Bonnie had been going to night school. She took courses in all sorts of subjects—drawing, painting, advertising, philosophy. "So many people in the clothing industry," she says, "seem to spend their whole lives with their own group. They work together. Their social activities are carried on together. They even get together to go to the Paris collections. I find one way to keep my interests broad is to study. I still go to night school regularly."

In one of her classes she met an art director, a man older and, Bonnie says, "much more sophisticated and better educated than I was." She married him not long afterward.

Her husband, who has since died, taught Bonnie a good deal, she thinks, about color and design, about understanding and appreciating art in all its phases. "What I learned from him was also an important part of my education," she says.

As an inevitable result of her growth Bonnie began to feel, after she had been with Adler & Adler for some three years, that she was again "boxed-in." And when she received offers from two West Coast motion picture studios, each of which invited her to join its staff of designers, she felt tempted to accept one of them. She wanted a change. She liked the idea of being near her family again. She felt the need of a new challenge. So in 1943 she went to Hollywood as a designer for Twentieth Century-Fox.

The new work was challenging indeed. For one thing,

Hollywood designers were not limited by wartime restrictions. If Bonnie wanted to use twelve yards of material for a single costume, there was no law which prevented her doing so. This fact alone gave her a sense of freedom and release.

She also loved doing so many different kinds of things, one after the other. Her first assignment was to design the fashionable modern clothes worn in the film, *Laura*—but shortly afterward she was doing period costumes for *Anna and the King of Siam* and *A Tree Grows in Brooklyn*. For each of these latter pictures she did weeks of the kind of costume research she so much enjoys. "I studied for months in the wonderful library on the film studio lot before I even began *Anna*," she remembers. "I loved doing that picture. I've always been strongly influenced by the Orient anyway. It seems to me that Oriental clothes have a kind of simplicity and elegance and beauty that is applicable to our life in this hemisphere today." How well she caught and expressed that kind of simple elegance in her costumes was proved to her when that film started a country-wide trend toward the oriental feeling in women's fashions.

A Tree Grows in Brooklyn was another of her favorites, although she remembers that some of her friends said, "But there aren't any real costumes in it. All the characters just wear those old gingham dresses." Betty Smith, however, author of the novel from which the film had been made, appreciated fully what Bonnie had achieved. "Everybody in the picture," she told the designer, "looks exactly the way I had always imagined them to look."

"It was exciting work," Bonnie herself says. "I wasn't designing for fashion, but for characteristics—which is the way I still like to design clothes for daily wear. I like to design clothes for a woman who plays a particular role in life, not simply to design clothes that follow a certain trend, or that express some new silhouette. That's why I like to keep learning all I can. You can't design a woman's clothes for her role in life if you don't know what that role is—don't understand the various roles various women play in the world today."

The lessons in speed which Bonnie had learned during her early days at the Roxy Theater proved both a benefit and a disadvantage to her at the studio. Company executives got in the habit of saying, "Let's give this picture to Cashin. We're in a hurry on it and we know Cashin will get it done." She was constantly plunging into new scripts, rushing through a whole batch of sketches and overseeing their reproduction. "I loved reading the scripts," Bonnie says. "I read them all— whether I was working on them or not."

But in the torrent of pictures whose costumes flowed through her workroom, not all were as interesting to her as *Anna and the King of Siam* or *A Tree Grows in Brooklyn.* Designing clothes at breakneck speed for one run-of-the-mill picture after another allowed her imagination little scope, and finally Bonnie began to have that "boxed-in" feeling once more.

"My years in Hollywood were wonderful years," she says now. "They were an important step in my development. I feel that every step I've ever taken has always been in the right direction, whether I knew it at the time or not, and that one certainly was. It made me more tolerant, for one thing. Before that I'd been something of a perfectionist—

impatient, for example, if a design I worked out didn't emerge from the complicated process of manufacturing in exactly the shape I had first dreamed it. But when I saw movie people start out with a magnificent idea, and when I watched all the things that could happen to that good idea to warp it and vitiate it, it taught me to accept the fact that these things happen, that people have to learn to work together in spite of them. And of course I learned an enormous amount about clothes too—clothes of all periods: how they went together, what their advantages were, what they could offer to us for our lives today."

Nevertheless by 1948 she was feeling a strong urge to get away. "It seemed to me that the whole wide world was out there, waiting to be explored," she says. "I decided I wanted most to go to Europe, so I just took a couple of months off, packed up my paint box and went."

It was the first of the many trips she has taken since— trips which have taught her, among other things, that traveling clothes must be the least of a traveler's worries, must suit themselves with the minimum of fuss and bother to a nomad who wants to devote every moment to strange sights and strange experiences, and no time at all to the problem of maintaining an elaborate wardrobe.

When she returned to the United States, refreshed and eager for new and stimulating work, she went back to the West Coast just long enough to finish out her contract there, and then she traveled eastward again to New York. Several offers awaited her, including one from her former employers, Adler & Adler. Bonnie studied them all. She also considered briefly the possibility of starting her own business. "But I'd have needed partners for that—somebody to put up the money—and the more I saw of the various people who might have become my partners, the less I thought of the idea," she says. Her final decision was to work once more for the company she had left some six years earlier.

Once more, but even more spectacularly this time, her first collection was a success. She thinks now that this was because her work in Hollywood had enabled her to maintain flexibility. Designers who had continued to work in New York throughout the war years, confined by wartime regulations, had not yet, she thinks, recovered from that experience.

"All those clothes of mine were perfectly simple," she says now. "They were simply the kind of clothes I liked to wear myself." But they caused a furor in the market. They were credited with establishing a completely new casual look for the American woman. That year Bonnie received, to her own amazement, both the Fashion Critics Award and the Neiman-Marcus Award for her original contribution to the field of American fashion design.

That outstandingly fresh collection had been, as the fashion writers all said, a breeze that stirred the stale air of the whole industry. The enthusiasm over it inevitably marked Bonnie as the producer of precisely the kind of clothes she had showed that first season. When she wanted to move on, the next season, to another kind of collection that she hoped would be equally fresh, she found that she was expected instead to produce near-duplicates of her original designs.

This attitude on the part of manufacturers is, she understands, widespread throughout the apparel industry, but even today it amazes her as much as it did then. At the time it made her feel "boxed-in once more—pigeonholed right where I was." She concluded that it was time to let go again, but again she didn't know what her next move ought to be.

Three offers were made to her as soon as it became known that she was contemplating a change. Bonnie Cashin, double prize-winner, was no longer an anonymous designer to the buyers who frequented the Seventh Avenue showrooms.

"But I felt," Bonnie says, "that none of the offers was exactly right for me. Each of them, I thought, would make me feel boxed-in again very soon. So that's when I decided to try to work out my own plan."

She would try to design, she decided, the clothes she wanted to design—coats, suits, dresses, special purpose garments—no matter what they were. They would not all be expensive; they would not all be low-priced. "The kind of girl I'm interested in," Bonnie points out, "will spend a lot, or a little, depending on the item she's buying and its value in her life. She may be willing to spend a good deal for a long-wearing all-season coat—but she may want a raincoat for only a few dollars." Bonnie realized, therefore, that no two of the garments she wanted to design would necessarily fit into any one manufacturer's cost-and-labor setup.

If she designed a coat that would have to be sold at a high price, she realized she would have to have it manufactured by a company already specializing in clothes of that general price range. If she designed an inexpensive raincoat, she would have to have it made up by a house that knew all the best ways to produce raincoats that could be sold inexpensively. But she was ready to assume part of the financial risk her plan entailed, along with the laborious details involved in

146

working with several manufacturers. She was willing to be paid on a royalty basis, much as an author is paid for his books: she would receive a percentage of the profit made on each garment sold. If her designs were not successful, she would suffer along with the manufacturer. But if her system worked out well, its end-result would be complete Bonnie Cashin wardrobes planned to meet all the various needs of an active woman's life.

The kind of customer to whom Bonnie thinks her clothes most appeal wants a wardrobe "of carefully balanced simplicity, spiked with all kinds of gay accessories." About seventy-five percent of the items in that wardrobe would probably be what Bonnie calls "timeless." The rest would be "frosting." But she does not believe that the clothes usually classified as staple—the completely classic suit, for example— are necessarily the timeless ones. "The beautifully made, individually styled thing which you might think of as a luxury is very likely to be the constant friend in your wardrobe year after year," she says. "Or that elegantly simple coat in the odd color—not classic in the common sense—may be your perennial favorite if it does something for you."

She knows enough about the apparel industry as a whole to understand why she could produce such wardrobes only by following her own plan. "Born a bit earlier," she once wrote of herself, at the request of a magazine editor, "and perhaps in another country, my niche would have been *couture*. In America, with its fabulous and excellent mass-production methods, this sort of thing has not been generally encouraged. Usually one must specialize in a defined category, a price line, or volume setup, and the labor wheels are geared to that. This is understandable and its virtues are many. The one vice is that it is apt to smother the creative root which provides oil for all those wheels. I realize that no one manufacturer can produce the diversified clothes I feel are needed for today's complex activities. So—if I can't change the industry, I can try to change my own working methods. How to combine the abilities of the artist with efficient production, and do this successfully, is the real problem."

She has not entirely solved the problem yet. Some of the first arrangements she made with manufacturers proved unsatisfactory for one reason or another. In one case a manufacturer thought Bonnie's designs were so unusual that they would not sell in large quantities, and should therefore be luxury-priced at a figure above the one he charged for his own standard products. The new high price frightened his regular customers. And other buyers, who might have been willing to pay it because they would have appreciated Bonnie's ideas, were not in the habit of visiting this particular showroom. "It takes time and effort to attract a new and different clientele," Bonnie says. But this particular manufacturer was impatient over the lack of immediate results, and Bonnie's contract with him was canceled.

A year or two later, however, Bonnie's creative innovations for that house were being copied in low-priced adaptations all over the country. Even the manufacturer for whom she had originally designed them was making and selling such adaptations in large quantities. But Bonnie—because her contract was no longer in effect, and because there is no legal protection against the "pirating" of a designer's work—received no payment at all from any of the businessmen who were profitably mass-producing those versions of her work.

"I've already 'given away' a good deal of my work for reasons of that kind," she says. "Trying to function on a free-lance basis, as I'm doing, requires a knowledge of business methods that I've never had a chance to acquire—a knowledge I'm going to need if my plan is to prove financially feasible. The money I've lost so far has shown me that. It has also proved to me what I've always suspected: that the road of the non-conformist is a tough one."

But the new plan has given her far more freedom than she ever experienced as a clothes designer in the past. She does not yet work in all fields—does not yet produce the complete wardrobes toward which she is aiming—but she has already done, among other things, lingerie, at-home clothes, raincoats, knit wear, sportswear, suits and coats and a variety of fashions made of suedes and leathers. And in each of those categories she has produced clothes which have won enormous acclaim and popularity. They have introduced new *ways* of dressing, because—as one fashion authority put it—Bonnie Cashin "does not design a line as such, but rather new items which are ever-responsive to changing trends and requirements." For example, she likes to design a coat that a woman will use all the year round as she travels from one climate to another in today's swift patterns of work and recreation.

Coats, as a matter of fact, are among Bonnie's special enthusiasms. She gives them plenty of pockets, including even back pockets such as the ones she used on her famous "tote jacket." One of her most successful was the alpaca-lined monk-collared coat that eventually was made up in both short and long versions, and in such materials as cotton element cloth and leather. Because it was as tough as it was chic it was reproduced so widely that it earned the reputation of being a fashion Ford, one of those ubiquitous garments that appear everywhere and seem at home wherever they go.

Another popular expression of Bonnie's feeling that coats should be able to go anywhere, any time, and with anything, is the group of rain-or-shine coats she has designed. The idea that a raincoat should be a drab and unflattering protection against bad weather has been out-dated ever since Bonnie Cashin proved that it could instead be frankly gay, as pretty on a starry night as it is useful in a downpour.

Her own lifelong hobby of knitting also prompted her to devise a whole new array of knitted suits and dresses which caused a great stir when they first appeared and which started a long-lasting enthusiasm for a new kind of knitted wear. Out of the idea that modern machine-knitted goods could be as versatile as woven fabric she created tailored and dressmaker suits and dresses unlike anything that had ever been available before except in expensive hand-knits. But she made certain her new garments were practical before she tried to market them. She made some up for herself, first of all, and wore them on a rugged cross-country automobile trip. Not until that trip was over, and she was convinced that the clothes would not sag and would be comfortable and wearable under a variety of conditions, was she ready to put them into production.

Her leather and suede fashions also created an enthusiasm that would last a long time. She made leather shirts and skirts, coats and slim-yoked breeches that became a favorite with seasoned travelers and devotees of country living. She matched specially dyed suedes to gabardine, to silk and to linen, to create outfits that had usefulness and an air of casual elegance.

Bonnie herself proved how a few of her leather garments and several of her knitted things could add up to a nearly complete wardrobe, when a friend wrote to ask her what she planned to take along on a painting-and-sightseeing journey to Greece. "I'll take a big overcoat of black goatskin to use all the time, day and evening," the designer wrote back. "I'll add a bell-shaped skirt to match and a camel-tan shirt. The shirt I can use as such, or as a light jacket over a knit sheath. My knits will be a scoop-neck dinner one in black, a three-piece in brown and black basque stripes which with its jacket is for daytime wear and without it is for evening; a hooded 'shell' sweater in bright yellow, and three other sweaters— a black, a white and a pinky-red low-necked one. I may also take my turtle-neck heavy shaker knit sheath—either the black or the red one. I have an overskirt of black satin, lined with pink, quite full and pretty to dance in. I'll take this, too, and wear it right over the knit evening sheath or with a low-necked sweater."

The common-sense quality of this travel-wise wardrobe is echoed in a very different kind of "wardrobe" which Bonnie invented for a hospitalized friend and which was later made up in quantities by a lingerie house. She had originally intended to buy for the friend a ready-made bed jacket, but all the ones she found in the shops seemed to her both dull and overelaborate. "They were all ruffled," she says, "and it occurred to me that ruffles would get awfully mussy in an

151

hour or so." So she made up a jacket of plaid gingham, unruffled but gay. And then she made a pillow slip to match it, with a huge pocket in one corner big enough to hold a supply of cleansing tissues and half a dozen of the other odds and ends that bedridden patients like to have ready at hand.

This little "Sitting Pretty" gift package, as it was named, illustrates again Bonnie Cashin's approach to her work: she designs from *need*. The need may be a practical one, or it may be of another variety. "Clothes that are right and beautiful—that are completely satisfying—fill an emotional need," Bonnie points out. And to design-from-need requires what she calls a strongly developed "sense of today."

This conviction is at the root of the advice she gives to young people who hope to become designers.

"Go out and live a while," she tells them. "Move around, work, travel, entertain, watch other people, learn about the world you live in—and then you'll know what kind of clothes you and other people need for it. Of course everybody dreams of designing beautiful ball gowns," she admits. "But in our lives today how often does anyone use such things? I love them myself, and the clothing industry has a few big balls a year where I actually get a chance to wear that kind of dress. But just 'going dancing' calls for other simpler kinds of clothes these days. And I don't know how any of us can design clothes that can be *lived* in without knowing a good deal about living."

Her own life is a very busy one—dealing with the several manufacturers with whom she works, sketching or draping her designs in the big many-windowed studio of her penthouse

152

apartment, traveling, studying, re-doing the barn-studio-house she recently acquired in the country north of New York, entertaining a crowd of friends at a salad, supper on her terrace. She likes best to plan those suppers for warm summer nights when her guests can look out over Manhattan's lights toward the Hudson River in one direction and the breeze-swept bay in another.

But Bonnie has discovered that her two-story penthouse— living room on one floor, bedroom-studio above—has a misleading effect on embryonic designers. Once, not long ago, she was asked to speak to a class of students visiting New York from an out-of-town design school, and she invited them to her studio. The young people were impressed the moment they stepped out of the elevator. The walls of the stairs they climbed were papered with Bonnie's sketches, splashed in color across sheets of newsprint, with rows of photographs of the philosophers, artists, scientists and musicians Bonnie particularly admires, with colorful bits of handcraft she has picked up on her travels. They grew wide eyed when they stepped into her living room, with its huge uncurtained window set in a wide gold picture frame, its view of the tree-planted terrace outside and the skyscrapers of midtown Manhattan beyond. And when she led them up one more flight to her studio, with its big neat desk, its walls festooned with multicolored native straw hats from many lands, its pillow-strewn couches, they were speechless with admiration—except for one girl. That young woman said earnestly, "It must be perfectly wonderful to be a famous designer, living like this in a penthouse!"

"I nearly glared at her," Bonnie admits. " 'Wonderful!'

I said to her. 'Have you any idea of the amount of hard work I've had to live through before I could afford this penthouse? Not that I don't enjoy it—I love it up here. But I've lived in considerably less attractive places in my time. And no matter where I live I work hard. Designing *is* hard work, you know—real work. So unless you're willing to accept that fact right now, you might as well stop thinking you'll ever be a designer yourself some day.' "

Looking toward her own future Bonnie knows that there is still plenty of work ahead. "I've still got a lot of planning to do," she says. "I still don't know whether my present scheme will be as satisfactory as I hope it will be. But somehow I'm certain that the most exciting, most productive years of my life are still ahead of me. I've got all sorts of things I want to do and I can't wait to try them all out. And I will try them all some day, too, because I'll never again let myself get boxed-in. I think by now I've learned pretty well when to let go."

Lorraine & Bard Budny

HUSBAND-AND-WIFE TEAMS, THOUGH NOT UN-usual in the entertainment world and in other arts and professions, have been rare in the apparel industry—so rare, in fact, that special interest was aroused by announcements mailed out early in 1955 inviting buyers and fashion magazine editors to

SEE OUR NEW COLLECTION OF
SUMMER SPORTSWEAR
DESIGNED FOR CHANGEABLE CLIMATES
BY
LORRAINE BUDNY
(*MLLE*. AWARD WINNER 1953)
PLUS A COMPANION GROUP OF
MEN'S SHIRTS AND SHORTS
BY
BARD BUDNY

155

But the Budnys' story is not included here because their married partnership is unique. It has another and wider interest as the case history of a new enterprise in a field where the mortality rate of new enterprises is extremely high.

Opening a new apparel house demands courage and a wide background of experience in the clothing industry. Lorraine and Bard both had the necessary courage. But it was Lorraine alone who had the particular experience that their undertaking demanded. She began to collect it some years before she even knew Bard Budny. She began—or at least attempted to begin—when she was a little girl named Lorraine Girouard.

The town of Chicopee, Massachusetts, where Lorraine was born, is an industrial center populated largely by families of French descent. Her parents were both French. She spoke their language before she could speak English. Most classes in the parochial school she attended were taught in French.

Lorraine's father, an industrial designer, had died even before his little daughter entered school. His young widow remarried several years later. Lorraine was still only eight years old when her stepfather lost his automobile business during the early days of the 1929 crash and the family decided to move westward. They settled on a 375-acre farm on Walled Lake, Michigan, where her stepfather organized a cattle "finishing" project: every year he traveled to the cattle-range country and brought back hundreds of steers to be fattened for the market on his rolling pasture land.

Lorraine's closest companion on the farm was a pet lamb which learned to follow her faithfully, in proper nursery-rhyme tradition. She attended a one-room country school that lay a mile and a half from her farmhouse home. In spite of the fact that neither her fellow-students nor her teacher could understand the tongue that was most familiar to Lorraine, she loved her new life. Today when she talks knowledgeably about grassland farming, and looks ahead to the day when she and Bard will raise cattle and horses of their own on the farm they recently acquired in Connecticut, she is proving how completely at home she became in that Michigan environment.

But one day when she read a story in a Sunday newspaper supplement, she realized that she would not be content to remain on a Michigan cattle farm forever. The story told of a Frenchman, Paul Poiret, who was a designer of women's clothes—clothes so beautiful that they drew admirers and purchasers from all over the world to his Paris salon. He was very wealthy and very famous, and other wealthy and famous people begged for the privilege of attending his fabulous parties. Lorraine made up her mind, right then and there, that she wanted to live exactly the kind of life Poiret lived, and that therefore she too would become a designer of clothes.

She would have liked to start studying for her career immediately, but the curriculum of her high school was not geared to students with Lorraine's particular ambition. It was organized for the benefit of boys who would be farmers when they grew up, and girls who would be farmers' wives. Animal husbandry, for example, was a compulsory course.

On the school principal's advice she chose home economics as her major. Her freshman and sophomore years would be concentrated upon cooking, but thereafter she would have two years of sewing courses. So Lorraine studied nutrition and home-canning, and learned dozens of recipes, and looked forward to becoming a junior and taking her first real steps toward a career as a designer. She had just finished her sophomore year when the family moved back east again, to St. Albans, Vermont, and then a few months later to Manchester, New Hampshire.

The best thing about the Manchester High School, Lorraine discovered, was that it offered a class in art. There, too, home economics remained her major because it was the only available one that was even remotely connected with the career she had decided upon. Students in that course, like those in the agricultural high school she had previously attended, were given two years of cooking and two years of sewing. But here the schedule was reversed; sewing was taught in the freshman and sophomore years—the years Lorraine had already completed. For that reason she still had not had a single lesson in sewing, had still not learned anything about making clothes, when financial reasons forced her to leave school during her junior year in order to go to work.

She took the first job she could find, as a general assistant to a commercial photographer. "I just did chores," she says. She worked at it until her family made its fifth move, this time to New York. The new location seemed ideal to Lorraine. Now, she thought, she could get the training she needed. She went immediately to the Traphagen School of Fashion and signed up for a sketching course.

"That was a mistake," she says now. "I should have studied draping instead. It's nice to be able to draw clothes, but sketching is not a basic tool of designing. Draping clothes—

158

being able to construct them—is."

She realized later how fortunate it was that she had to carry on her work at Traphagen during the evenings and devote her days to earning a living, and that she decided to get a job as a salesclerk in a women's wear department. She still thinks that handling clothes day in and day out, and dealing with customers, is a good way to learn something about the apparel industry.

"But I didn't know how to go about getting a job," she says. "So I just sat down and wrote letters to the six department stores whose names I knew best. I told all of them exactly the kind of work I wanted to do, and why." Every one of those letters brought a reply from a store personnel department, but only the personnel head of Russek's invited Lorraine to come in for an interview. "Would you be willing to start as a stock girl?" she was asked.

It was not what she had hoped for, but Lorraine accepted. A stock girl at least had the opportunity to handle endless quantities of dresses, suits and coats, even if she never saw them being fitted and never heard a customer say why she liked one garment better than another. Lorraine had been on her new job for two weeks, and was carefully putting away the dresses that had been worn in one of the store's regular fashion showings, when her tall well-carried figure, her smooth brown hair and wide brown eyes, caught the eye of David Nemerov, later president of Russek's. "Why don't we make a model out of that girl?" Nemerov said. He told Lorraine to try on one of the dresses she had just hung up and to walk across the room in it.

"The dress happened to fit me in all the right places,"

Lorraine says, "and I guess I managed the walk all right."

Within a few minutes she had ceased to be a stock girl and had become, instead, a Russek's model.

Like other designers whose background has included a spell of modeling, Lorraine knows what valuable training it can be. She thinks she encountered another stroke of luck shortly afterward when another Russek's model, who also worked in the wholesale dress houses, introduced Lorraine to Paul Parnes and helped her land a job modeling for that well-known designer. Lorraine felt then that she was at last making real progress toward her goal.

That goal was no longer her first childish desire to become a designer in order to lead a glamorous life. The actual designing interested her now, and she knew that this demanded a high degree of knowledge and a variety of skills, in addition to pure creative ability. Some of that knowledge and some of those skills could be learned, she realized, in just such a job as she had, if she watched closely all that went on around her in the Parnes workroom.

Lorraine continued to study while she worked for Parnes, and when she finished her course at Traphagen she began a life class at an art school. "That one was important," she points out. "We had to learn about anatomy—the placement and movement of bones and muscles. If you want to design clothes properly you certainly have to know something about the human bodies that are going to wear them."

During the slow season at Parnes she did additional modeling at Sak's—a belated result of the letters she had written to those six department stores—and also showed custom wear at Sophie's exclusive establishment. She was so successful a model that when the Parnes designer left that firm at the end of Lorraine's first year there, he took her along with him to the larger house of Adler & Adler.

Lorraine was still officially a model but she had been trying her hand at sketching original designs, and one day Louis Adler himself looked at some of her drawings. "Bonnie Cashin is going to need an assistant very soon," he said. "How would you like to work for her?"

Bonnie Cashin, who was on the West Coast at the time, was then doing the first of her two stints for Adler & Adler. Her name was not yet as well established as it would be later, but already her creative thinking had won the admiration of almost everybody inside the industry. Lorraine herself enormously admired the Cashin approach to clothes, and eagerly welcomed the chance to serve as a sort of Girl Friday to that particular designer.

"When Bonnie got back from California she agreed to take me on," Lorraine says. "And I'll never forget that the first thing she asked me to do was to match a certain color. It didn't occur to her to wonder whether I knew enough about paints to be able to achieve the shade. She always assumed that if she could do a thing herself, everybody could do it—as if she thought she had no special abilities herself. She was wonderful to work for."

During the two years Lorraine remained on that job she learned, she says, a great deal about color. "And I also learned," she adds, "a great deal about the organization of the whole design process: how to plan a theme for a collection, then to choose the colors for it, then the fabrics, and finally to work out the individual designs. There are other organizational plans for the same process, of course, but I still follow that one myself today."

After Bonnie Cashin left New York to work as a motion picture designer, Lorraine remained at Adler & Adler. She was already doing some designing on her own, and her things won considerable praise. On the strength of them she obtained a position as a full-fledged designer with the house of Davidow, long famous for its classically tailored suits and dresses.

"But I wasn't ready for that step," Lorraine says now. "It was too soon for me to tackle that much on my own." After only six months at Davidow she was glad to leave for a new job that would give her more of the experience she thought she needed. The opportunity came to her through Adolph Klein, who had been a salesman for Parnes when Lorraine worked there, and who had since opened his own house, Townley Frocks. The Townley designer was Claire McCardell, one of the first American fashion creators whose name became widely known to the public.

"I modeled for her," Lorraine says. "And, because she had so many things to attend to, I gradually took over all sorts of odds and ends during the year and a half I was there. I sold in the showroom—selling is one of the things I like least, even now—and I handled her publicity, which was growing all the time."

It was probably the quality of Claire McCardell's publicity, as Lorraine managed it, which prompted a friend to recommend Lorraine to the personnel executive at Lord & Taylor. At any rate she suddenly found herself being offered a job as assistant buyer in the better suits department of that store.

"I felt I really hadn't been getting very far toward being a designer," Lorraine recalls. "I thought maybe I never would—that I ought to go into merchandising instead." But at the end of a year at Lord & Taylor she knew definitely that merchandising wouldn't really satisfy her. She was thinking of leaving the store altogether when the merchandise manager invited her to serve as what he called "director of fashion promotion." So for another year—an especially important year, because that was when she and Bard Budny were married—Lorraine remained with Lord & Taylor, promoting its new Young New Yorker shop, taking care of newspaper publicity, managing special fashion shows such as the one that marked the opening of Lord & Taylor's new store in a Westchester suburb.

Again the quality of the publicity she prepared earned her a reputation. When *Harper's Bazaar* was looking for an associate editor Lorraine was offered the job.

"I was all right at visiting the various dress houses and selecting things to be featured in the magazine," she says. "But I wasn't much good at the photography sittings that were part of my work. I was always too much interested in the clothes themselves—I didn't understand enough about the making of a good fashion photograph.

"And suddenly," Lorraine says, "I realized I was way off the track. I was getting farther and farther away from designing, which I was still convinced was really what I wanted to do, if I possibly could. So I thought I'd better get busy and do something."

What she did was to apply for a designing job with a firm which had an opening at the time, only to be told that her things were "too extreme" for that particular house. Lorraine walked unhappily out of the manufacturer's office and then, before she left that floor of the building—it was one of the big Seventh Avenue skyscrapers devoted entirely to the apparel industry—she stopped in on impulse to see the brother of the man she had just interviewed. The brother, Rubin Goodman, owner of the house of Sportwhirl, offered to hire Lorraine on the spot. She accepted the offer, although she knew that Goodman's previous designers had been retained only long enough to complete a single collection.

"But he was willing to let me do as I pleased," Lorraine says gratefully. If the experience was valuable to her, she proved equally valuable to her employer. She remained at Sportwhirl for four years. By the end of that time it was a far better-known house than it had been when she arrived. It was so well known, in fact, that young Jeanne Campbell was delighted to take Lorraine's place there when Lorraine finally left to return to Adler & Adler. Bonnie Cashin had just resigned after her second period of work for that house, in order to inaugurate her free-lance business, and Lorraine was invited to design Adler & Adler's next collection.

While Lorraine worked she was watching Bonnie Cashin's career with eager interest. After completing one new collection for Bonnie's and her own former employers, and designing dresses and separates for a short time thereafter for Sportlane Deb, a junior house, Lorraine too decided to become a freelance designer.

"I didn't have the same setup Bonnie uses," she says. "I worked on a retainer system. I signed up with a sportswear house, a dress house, a maker of raincoats, and a sweater-and-skirt house, and did work for all of them for a flat annual fee paid by each manufacturer." For each house she selected fabrics, supervised the sample-making and handled promotion, in addition to doing the actual designing.

That was the year *Mademoiselle* magazine gave her its merit award in design. "Mrs. Budny has a wonderful feeling for fabrics," the magazine's citation noted, reminding its readers of her coating-weight skirts and her fleece-and-leather coats. It also credited Lorraine with chalking up "firsts" for her keg jacket, her use of rib knit in combination with tweed and jersey, and her dramatic collars or cuffs of black fox fur on simple otherwise unadorned dresses.

"I was able to keep my four-ring circus going all right," Lorraine says of that period, "and I was making a satisfactory amount of money, but the system didn't give me the greater freedom I had expected from it. Instead of doing the kind of things I wanted to do, I found myself pressed more and more into doing exactly the kind of things each of my manufacturers had made in the past and wanted to go on making. So in that respect the whole thing wasn't working out very well.

"That's when I decided to try to start my own business," she goes on. "I'd saved money and I thought I could swing it. So I talked it over with Bard and he said, 'Why don't I come in with you?' and I said, 'Why don't you?'"

Bard Budny had been, for some time, a successful businessman and the executive vice-president of a large baking company. Of course there are a good many men in the apparel industry today whose interests are purely a businessman's, and who speak in terms of costs and labor and profits rather than fabric and color and line. "But that's not the kind of businessman Bard is," Lorraine says.

With his mother and older sister Budny had come to this country from Russia at the age of three. His Cossack-soldier father was then a prisoner of war in Japan, and did not join the family until later. Bard loved horses—once, briefly, he raised Morgan stallions in Vermont—and for a time he thought he would train to be a doctor, but he abandoned both these enthusiasms to become a chemical engineer, an expert in yeasts and fermentations.

Even as an expert in one specific line, however, Bard Budny retained a wide assortment of other interests. During World War II, for example, before he did active service, he was asked to help solve the pressing problem of obtaining enough bakers to staff the troop ships that were steadily plying back and forth across the Atlantic. He organized and wrote a course of lessons in baking—and trained 16,000 bakers in sixteen weeks.

Often during his subsequent technical work for one of the big breweries, and later for the baking company, he designed machinery to perform some new and highly complex process, or to speed up a process which had never before been performed efficiently. He was also skillful at handling labor negotiations and contracts.

"He's good with his hands, too," Lorraine says. "He's built most of the furniture for our New York apartment. But along with that, and all the other things he's done, he's always been interested in clothes. He used to sketch special kinds of things he wanted for himself and ask me to get them made up in my workroom—as if we had nothing else to do except run

166

up extra items like a man's shirt in our spare time!"

So Lorraine was not too surprised when Bard Budny said, "Why don't I come in with you?" and then resigned his vice-president's job (though he agreed to go on serving the baking industry as a labor relations consultant and to devote some time to its technical problems). Their new apparel house was formally organized under the firm name of Lorraine Budny, Inc., in the autumn of 1954.

Asked to explain exactly how their business developed from an idea into an actual going concern, Lorraine says, "We had to figure it out for ourselves, step by step. There is no textbook available on how to start this kind of a business."

They decided that the first thing to do was to acquire a location for their showroom and workrooms.

"We looked at the big Seventh Avenue buildings," Lorraine says. "Of course it would have been fine to open at 498 Seventh, or 530 Seventh, or at one of the other famous addresses in the wholesale district. But space at those places is very expensive. It seemed to us that it would be better to start out small, and hope to expand, than to start out too big and perhaps have to back down later on. So we looked along the side streets off Seventh Avenue and we found the rentals there about half the price of those in the big Avenue buildings."

The place they chose was only half a block from Seventh, on 38th Street. It included a sizable showroom, an office, a dressing room for models, a tiny designers' studio, and a room big enough to accommodate several sewing machines, long tables for the making of samples and patterns, and plenty of space where clothes could be stocked and packed for shipment.

"But the most important thing we had to do in the beginning was to find a good patternmaker," Lorraine says, "because the best-designed clothes in the world are worthless if they don't fit the customer. Translating sketches or original draped models into a perfect size 12, for example, and making up the patterns for all the other sizes in which that garment is going to be produced, is a very specialized process and one that must be done well if a dress house is going to succeed. We're very lucky. The woman we hired originally as a sample hand has proved to be a remarkably good patternmaker."

Lorraine Budny's designs, incidentally, are usually made up in sizes which are slightly smaller in the waist and slightly larger in the hips than the standard sizes issued by the government for the guidance of clothes manufacturers. "Most designers make some tiny adjustments of their own in these measurements," Lorraine explains. "I happen to think my clothes look best on girls who have smaller-than-normal waists and whose hips may be a little larger than the standard. That's why my things deviate as they do."

The Budnys' opening took place in February of 1955. Their showroom was gayly pink-and-white, with screens Bard had made out of old shutters cut down, fitted together and painted white. They themselves greeted buyers, and the fashion editors who had come to see their things. Their first collection included summery dresses and separates, and the men's shirts and shorts which Bard had designed. "We use the same materials for the men's and women's things," Lorraine says, "but that's about as far as we usually go in the his-and-her direction.

"Bard sketches his designs and tells us exactly how he

168

wants them made up," she explains. "Occasionally I have to say that a certain effect he wants is impossible and he insists upon knowing why. He's learning very quickly why some things are technically possible and others aren't. When we were in Jamaica last year he had a tailor there make up, to his specifications, a pair of shorts that I liked so well I copied them for my own group of women's shorts."

Work on filling the orders that resulted from their first showing began immediately after those orders were placed. Delivery on schedule is an important aspect of success in the apparel industry.

Lorraine herself did the "marker job"—the laying out of patterns on lengths of material in such a way that the least possible waste occurs. Poor markers can run a dress house into bankruptcy; good ones can save pennies that quickly add up to profits.

The Budnys had already signed contracts with the manufacturers who, using Lorraine's marker and Lorraine's samples as a guide, would make up their clothes. The selection of those manufacturers had been based on several factors: the price each one quoted on specific items, his experience in clothes of the general kind the Budnys had designed, his reputation for good workmanship and reliable delivery, and his success at making up one trial copy, called a "duplicate," of each Budny sample submitted to him.

"Like most houses we use more than one manufacturer," Lorraine explains. "One may be best for soft things, another for more tailored clothes. You have to shop around to find the ones that will be most satisfactory for your own particular line.

"Of course the contract manufacturers are willing to make the markers themselves," she adds, "but I'd rather do my own, at least in the beginning. After all, a manufacturer is interested only in making a profit, and some of them try to do that by skimping slightly here and there. If I do the markers myself I know that every piece of every garment is just the size it ought to be. But I suspect Bard may take over the job very soon. He's fascinated by the technical aspects of it and has been hanging around the workroom learning how it's done. He was already cutting patterns some time ago. He's really started at the bottom of this business but he's moving up very quickly."

The materials which the Budnys send to their manufacturers therefore include the fabrics to be used in the garments, plus all buttons, zippers and trimmings, plus Lorraine's markers and the duplicates which the manufacturer has already made. When all those things have been shipped off the Budnys are free to tackle their designs for the next season, and to talk with the random customers who come in from time to time, perhaps to re-order, perhaps on a first curious visit to a new house they neglected to call on during its official showing weeks.

When the finished garments come back from the manufacturers, Lorraine and Bard superintend the inspection, and see to it that the right clothes are packed into the right cartons for delivery to their customers.

"I've always had a natural curiosity," Lorraine says, "and in all the many places where I've worked in the past I've watched the various operations that went on around me—including even the job of packing, which doesn't sound very exciting but which has to be properly done if clothes are to arrive in time and in good shape. Now my curiosity is paying off. Now I'm not only interested in every aspect of our business—which I have to be if we're to be successful—but I know something about all of them, from the construction of fabrics through the cutting of samples and the making of patterns, to promoting the finished merchandise."

Her knowledge of fabrics dates back at least to her days at Sportwhirl, where she showed such curiosity about the textiles she ordered that a fabric salesman invited her to visit his mill. Lorraine went, and later made a point of visiting other mills. Finally she bought her own loom and learned how to weave. "I've never really designed a new textile on the loom," she says, "but my weaving—which I must say I've neglected lately—has given me a pretty fair education in textiles and has been very useful to me."

Because of her past experience she is equally knowledgeable when it comes to promotion. She understands, for one thing, that each magazine settles upon a theme for a forthcoming issue before sending its editors into the field to study the new collections. The editors are therefore going to be interested chiefly in those clothes which fit that theme. If they offer to feature a particular designer's work it is not merely because they like it personally, but because it will serve to illustrate their editorial point of view.

"Sometimes, of course," Lorraine says, "a magazine will become so interested in a certain model—because it fits so well into the issue then being planned—that the editors will ask the designer to do something more along the same line. If they're planning a whole issue around beach-resort clothes, for example, and they happen to like a pair of shorts and a shirt I've designed, they might ask me to make it up in another fabric or two, or to design a matching dress, so that they could build a whole page around those items."

Some day the Budnys hope to increase their staff. At present Lorraine, who studied bookkeeping and stenography in high school, keeps the firm's financial records and types up all the publicity releases. She also possesses a salesman's first qualification—a wide acquaintance among store buyers, even though she doesn't much enjoy the showroom end of her business and is delighted that a general assistant she hired has a real flair for that job. She also hopes to have a cutter on the staff before long, so that they will not have to contract with their manufacturers to cut all garments from her marker. "And of course Bard will be handling all our contracts, and serving as production head, as soon as he becomes a little more at home in the business," she adds. "His background in labor and management problems is going to be very helpful to us."

Perhaps the most valuable asset Lorraine brings to her new business is awareness of its complexities. "We've tried to pick the best methods," she says, "but there's no real standard to judge by. There is no established practice, for example, on how to price a garment. Of course you figure your costs as closely as you can—your fabric, your labor, your overhead—but there are always hidden things you didn't count on. You just have to do the best you can." The wholesale price of their summer wear was from $5.75 to $12.75, and their fall things from $7.75 to $36.75, but they realize those rates may change as their business grows and adapts itself to their customers.

172

They are interested chiefly in dealing with small shops for both their men's and women's wear. "We both just like them," she says.

They both also instinctively design from need, with much the same feeling with which Bonnie Cashin approaches her work. One of Bard's shirts has sleeves and body all cut from one piece, because he himself finds this the most comfortable shape for active wear; and Lorraine, appreciating the value of that particular cut, made an adaptation of it for her own collection.

Among the things for which she has received special acclaim in the past are items which illustrate this attitude. Her "transition" fashions, which she defines as clothes that go on from season to season—such as a simple jersey sheath, for example—have a usefulness that is not cut short by the calendar. Her flat-flaring collarless wrap coats, which she designed after a trip to Egypt—the camel driver she and Bard hired to take them to the Pyramids wore similar garments—are also among these useful items that go on from one season into the next, and that therefore fill a dozen needs in a woman's wardrobe.

It always gives Lorraine a special sense of satisfaction to see clothes she designed years earlier still being worn by women who find them steadily useful. Her stovepipe jersey blouse, with its high collar that could lie flat or button up under the chin, became a fashion staple that lasted for years after she first offered it in one of her Sportwhirl collections. So did her pie-cut jersey blouse. Big-pocketed little jackets, which she designed during the same period, also were popular for a long time, as was her alpaca-on-the-outside jacket, a contrast to the earlier alpaca-lined one of other designers.

YOUNG FACES IN FASHION

Lorraine and Bard Budny have visited France and had a glimpse of the big Paris houses during the showing of their collections. She found them stimulating—just as she thinks Paris is now stimulated by American designers. "We all profit by each other," is the way she puts it. But her own inspirations derive from her daily life, and from the things she sees about her. The ideas with which she embellishes her translation of need-into-fashion come to her from all sorts of things.

"A cane chair seat once gave me an idea for a belt," she remembers. "And I used the hex signs I saw on Pennsylvania barns, combined with the lovely hand-painted designs on the dining room ceiling of our 1723 farmhouse, to decorate the sleeves of a group of blouses.

"I like to go through the art museums, too," she says. "I almost run through them—though I know that sounds silly. But every time I do that I see a color I've never noticed before. I catch sight of it out of the corner of my eye and suddenly I know it's a color I want to use. Of course I'm not talking now about visiting costume museums," she adds. "I go there for research. But I find my color ideas on those quick trips through picture galleries."

Sports cars gave her the idea for her pioneering sports car clothes. "After all," she says, "clothes ought to be designed in the same way cars are designed, or refrigerators. A refrigerator must be basically functional, but it ought also to enhance the kitchen where it stands. And cars must function efficiently, but we like them to be good-looking, too. In the same way, I think, clothes should be flattering to a woman as well as functional to her way of life."

174

Her own favorite clothes are sports clothes "that are as comfortable in town as they are in the country. Our working and our living are so closely meshed these days," she points out, "that our clothes must be acceptable for both. Nobody wants to have to change clothes each time he—or she—travels from a suburban house to an office, say, or drives out from the city on a Friday night for a country week end."

Her one exception to this philosophy of generally useful clothes is her attitude toward evening wear. "I think we ought to dress up more in the evenings," she says. "We ought to make a point then of wearing the sort of dress we definitely wouldn't wear to class or to the office, whether we're staying at home or going out. I even think parties should start later, and plays too, so that we would all have time to change into something really very pretty."

The Budnys' plans for the future include clearing the land on their farm so that someday they will be able to raise cattle and horses. They both like to cook and would like to be able to spend more time on the long-cooking Italian dishes they prefer—though Lorraine also likes certain French dishes and Bard occasionally reproduces the Russian meals he remembers from his boyhood. Lorraine would like to have more leisure to work at the writing she enjoys. And they would both like to travel more.

"But the difficulty is to find the time," Lorraine says. They both know there will be little leisure in their lives until their new business is well-established.

They know they have not chosen an easy road, and they expect it to be uphill for a long time to come. They like the road, though, and they do not mind having to make an effort in order to climb it. When people ask them how they manage to work together all day long, and still be able to find anything to talk about in the evening, Lorraine looks surprised. "Why, we talk about what we've been doing," she says. "We can sit in our little office all day, across the desk from each other, and each be so busy that we scarcely speak from one hour to the next. Naturally we have plenty to talk about in the evenings—that's the only time we get a chance to talk."

Perhaps husband-and-wife teams will become more frequent in the apparel industry now that Lorraine and Bard Budny have shown how effective such a team can be. It's even possible that some day, if their establishment grows as they hope it will and they acquire the leisure they look forward to, they'll combine their experience and their abilities to produce that textbook that is still lacking in their field: a textbook that will finally tell other beginners exactly how to start a new business like the Budnys' and how to make it succeed.